CU00701783

COSMOPOLITAN
Perfect Pasta

Also written by Richard Ehrlich and published by Robson Books

Cosmopolitan Meals in Minutes

COSMOPOLITAN
Perfect Pasta

Richard Ehrlich

 **Robson Books**

First published in Great Britain in 1997 by Robson Books
Ltd, Bolsover House, 5-6 Clipstone Street, London
W1P 8LE

Copyright © 1997 Richard Ehrlich and the National
Magazine Company
The right of Richard Ehrlich to be identified as author of
this work has been asserted by him in accordance with the
Copyright, Designs and Patents Act 1988

British Library Cataloguing in Publication Data
A catalogue record for this title is available from the British
Library

ISBN 1 86105 146 8

The expression Cosmopolitan is the trademark of The
National Magazine Company Limited and The Hearst
Corporation, registered in the UK and the USA, and other
principal countries of the world, and is the absolute
property of The National Magazine Company Limited and
The Hearst Corporation. The use of this trademark other
than with the express permission of The National Magazine
Company or The Hearst Corporation is strictly prohibited.

All rights reserved. No part of this publication may be
reproduced, stored in a retrieval system, or transmitted in
any form or by any means, electronic, mechanical,
photocopying, recording or otherwise, without the prior
permission in writing of the publishers.

Typeset in Bembo by Pitfold Design, Hindhead, Surrey.
Printed in Great Britain by St Edmundsbury Press Ltd,
Bury St Edmunds, Suffolk.

Contents

COSMOPOLITAN
Perfect Pasta

I could live without almost any food, but I couldn't live without pasta. For me it's the comfort food par excellence, soothing and filling and deeply reassuring. It's the perfect partner for almost any set of flavours, whether from Italian cuisine (the obvious choice) or French, Middle Eastern, Asian – really, just about anything from anywhere in the world. The basic ingredient has little flavour of its own, but it does have two things which are just as important: texture and bulk. Pasta-lovers like nothing more than the feel of the stuff between their teeth, and as long as the sauce is good, they will be in heaven.

Because the basic ingredient is so versatile, I cook it in all sorts of unusual ways, taking inspiration from all over the place. One chapter of the book is devoted to Asian-style recipes, since Asian cuisines are every bit as pasta-crazy as Italian. In the other chapters, certain ingredients appear and reappear constantly, especially tomatoes, garlic, bacon and fresh vegetables. I make no apologies for this: I would rather see home cooks concentrating on the foods they love than 'experimenting' with new ingredients which might not work out.

Having said that, however, I should immediately add that substitutions can easily be made for most of the sauce ingredients in these recipes. If you don't like courgettes (which I happen to adore), use whatever green vegetable is available – and whichever you happen to like. The important thing is to cook your pasta well, and to eat it in a spirit of enjoyment, whether you're dining alone, with your One True Love, or with a gang of friends and a case of good, cheap wine. Of all the ingredients you can combine with pasta, enjoyment is the only one that is always, and I mean *always,* indispensable.

Just as pasta itself is a wonderfully simple food, so too is the cooking of pasta a simple procedure. It takes just three elements: a pot, water, and salt. And even the salt may not be essential.

What definitely is essential is a good *cooking pot.* There are special pasta cookers you can buy with built-in straining inserts which lift out easily, thus allowing the cooking water to flow back into the pot. I own one of these pots (made by Lagostina), and I have to admit that it is a joy to use. You just stand there holding the insert over the pot until the water's drained out, then give the insert a final shake and tip the cooked pasta into your serving bowl.

Much as I love my pasta pot, however, I must also admit that it's a luxury (and it is rather expensive, more in the wedding-present league than everyday-purchase). Any large saucepan will do fine, or a stockpot, if you're cooking large quantities of pasta. (Note, however, that pasta for a big crowd will require a very big pot of boiling water, and handling it safely calls for Superman-style strength.) For smaller quantities, a smaller pot will do. Just remember that you need lots of water proportionally to the pasta if you're going to cook it right – but more about that in a moment.

Needless to say, if you don't use a special pasta pot you will need something to drain off the water from the cooked pasta. A sieve may suffice for small quantities but a *colander* is much better. Buy one that will sit in your sink without tipping over, and buy stainless steel or enamelled steel rather than plastic if possible.

That's all you need as far as equipment is concerned, though one of those special spaghetti servers may also be useful. They're cheap, and they work very well.

It constantly amazes me that so many people don't understand the role of *water* in cooking pasta. They half-fill a tiny little pot, put it on the hob, turn on the heat, then immediately tip in the pasta. The result is terrible: starchy and gluey pasta. But still they persist. Please, please, remember these principles:

1. Pasta needs a lot of water to cook well – around four litres per 500g (1lb 2oz) of dried pasta. This is because it absorbs a huge amount of water during cooking, and if there isn't enough in the pot it will end up being too starchy.
2. The water must be boiling rapidly when the pasta goes in.
3. You must stir the pasta for thirty seconds or so when it goes in, so that the pieces don't stick together as their outer layers of starch soften in the hot water.

4. The water must return to the boil as quickly as possible once the pasta's in.

If you follow these rules, your pasta will always cook right. It's as simple as that.

When you're really pressed for time, there are a few shortcuts that speed things up. The most time-consuming aspect of pasta cookery is waiting for the water to boil, and that wait can be a frustrating one. To hurry it along, do the following:

- Boil half the water you need in your saucepan and the remainder in the kettle. Or do the whole load in the kettle, transferring each kettleful to the pot as it's done. This is the fastest way to boil water.

- As soon as the kettle has boiled, pour it into the pot and boil another kettle. If your pot isn't a big one, the second kettle can be used to top up the water in the pot.

- Cover the pot as soon as the water starts to get hot: this is the only way to make water boil faster. Adding salt, sometimes thought to slow down boiling, makes no appreciable difference.

Incidentally, when draining the pasta it's a good idea to scoop out a spoonful and set it aside. If your sauce turns out to be on the dry side, you can add a little of this cooking water to thin it out.

Salt is the subject of some disagreement among pasta cooks. The old rule holds that you should salt the water, so that the pasta absorbs a little while cooking. It will never have the right amount of salt if it's seasoned with it afterwards, they say. And they think that every 500g (1lb 2oz) of pasta (dried weight) needs about 25ml (1½ tbsp) of salt in its cooking water.

But I know pasta manufacturers who say this simply isn't true. They think you can salt afterwards with perfectly good results. For the record, I add salt to the water after it's boiled and before the pasta goes in. But I suspect that it doesn't make a great deal of difference.

The fourth element in pasta cookery is *time,* and it's often the trickiest element for beginners. Pasta, as most people now realise, is at its best when cooked *al dente.* That's an Italian phrase meaning literally 'to the bite', and it refers to a quality of being chewably soft while still retaining some degree of resistance. Undercooked pasta is slightly crunchy or leathery in the mouth. Overcooked pasta is soft, slimy, squidgy and unappetising. Perfect pasta occupies the middle ground between those two extremes – and it's actually very easy to achieve once you've had a little practice.

Most packets of dried pasta specify a cooking time, and you should pay attention to those instructions. A small, thin pasta shape will cook faster than a thick one. But don't take the instructions on the packet as an immutable truth. Because it's so important not to overcook, you'll be safer if you set a timer for a minute or two less than the time given by the manufacturer. Test a single piece when the timer goes off, then pay close attention during the rest of the cooking. Don't leave the room, or get distracted. Stick with your pasta for that last crucial minute or two, so you won't find it's gone into overcook while your back was turned.

Some foods can be left after cooking very happily, to sit or rest for many minutes while other parts of the meal finish their spell on the hob or in the oven. Pasta is not one of them. Whenever possible, you should aim to sauce it and serve it immediately it's done. The two exceptions to this rule are pasta that's going to cook further (for example, in macaroni cheese) and pasta that's destined for a salad. There are special procedures for both those situations, and you'll find them in the appropriate chapters of this book.

If the pasta is to be served straight away but you have to leave it for some reason, two precautions are useful. One is to undercook it slightly, then rinse quickly under cold water and return it to the pot. You can then reheat it (and complete cooking) with the sauce mixed in. But this will only work if you are serving a very wet sauce, like the tomato sauce on page 114. Incidentally, there is no other reason to rinse cooked pasta. If you've cooked it in enough water, it will not be starchy or sticky – the usual reasons put forth for rinsing.

The second precaution is to drain it particularly well, then return it to the pot with a good knob of butter or a generous drizzle of olive oil. Toss well, then leave with the lid slightly ajar. This will hold the pasta for a few minutes – but no longer, please.

Fresh or Dried?

There's a lot of mystique attached to fresh pasta. Some people assume that fresh must be better than dried, just as fresh vegetables are assumed to be better than frozen. Well, that's not even a half-truth: it's more like a ten per cent truth. The whole truth is that fresh pasta hand-made by an expert will be better than just about any pasta anywhere in the world – but most fresh pasta that's sold commercially does not fit that description. Indeed, a lot of commercial fresh pasta is really pretty mediocre.

That's why I almost never use fresh pasta unless I have made it myself. And while pasta-making is fun, it's also something that I believe most busy home cooks just don't have time for. This is why all the recipes here are for plain old dried pasta, your choice of shape with a few exceptions. The only proviso is that the pasta must be *Italian, Italian*, or *Italian*. English-made pasta can be very good, Greek pasta is much more doubtful. Italian pasta is the best in the world. That's what I use, and it's what I think you should use too.

The only exception to the Italy-or-nothing rule comes in the recipes for dishes of non-European origin. Chinese and Japanese pasta is different from those made in the Italian style. Some are made with rice or other grains rather than wheat, and they tend to cook faster and feel different in the mouth. Nearly every supermarket now sells Chinese egg noodles and sometimes some of the Japanese noodles as well; specialist suppliers will have an even larger range of what's available from these countries. Most of the

Asian recipes here, however, confine themselves to Chinese egg noodles. Please do experiment with the others, using a good Chinese, Thai or Japanese cookbook as a guide.

How Much Do I Need?

This is a hard question to answer, but the general rule should be: make a lot. If you're entertaining, your friends should have plenty to eat. If you're cooking for yourself, make a little extra just in case you prove to be really hungry. Leftovers can be eaten the next day, and since the basic ingredient's so cheap, you have nothing to lose by being generous with quantities. Some cookery writers say that 50g (2oz) of uncooked pasta per person is the right amount, but I think they're dead wrong. For me, anything less than 100g (4oz) per person of dried pasta is just not enough. And I am rarely left with leftovers the next day. Of course, if you're serving pasta as a starter, in the traditional Italian manner, a smaller portion will do. But most of us nowadays serve it as a main course. Please, don't stint on quantities.

Pass the Cheese, Please

Some people serve grated Parmesan with every pasta dish they make. This is a mistake. Some pasta dishes would be useless without it, really and truly not worth eating. But some don't need it, and while the addition of cheese might not ruin the dish, neither will it improve it. Please pay attention to those recipes where I've indicated that cheese is not needed – and save your money for buying Parmesan where it's essential.

Speaking of Parmesan, I hope I don't need to say that there's only one way to buy this wonderful invention: in a piece, or freshly grated by a good Italian deli. Industrial manufacturers sell something that they call Parmesan in convenient little tubs. They might as well call it cheese-flavoured sawdust. The taste is negligible, the texture unappealing, the freshness gone. Not only that, it's expensive. Fresh Parmesan is also expensive – and the older and more flavourful, the more expensive it will be. But it is worth it. Please, *please* do not buy the stuff in tubs.

Rules – Who Needs 'em?

Apart from these few basic rules, the best rule about pasta cookery is not to think about any rules at all. Some of the most wonderful pasta dishes I have ever made resulted from accident rather than from a recipe or predetermined objective. Once you get into the habit of cooking the stuff, you will find that you can make delicious dishes using whatever you happen to have in your fridge, freezer and kitchen cupboards. The most important ingredients are good pasta and a flexible, willing mind. With those basics, you can't go wrong.

Almost Instant

Quasi Puttanesca Sauce
Quick Tomato and Garlic Sauce
Quick Spinach and Garlic Sauce
Smoked Salmon, Sour Cream and Chives
Caper Sauce
Tomato, Lemon and Basil Sauce
Sausage and Garlic Sauce
Pasta with Garlic, Chilli and Peas
Basic Cream Sauce
Creamy Sun-dried Tomato Sauce
Creamy Prosciutto Sauce
Olive and Chilli Sauce
Herb Sauce
Quick Tuna Sauce
Sun-dried Tomato Sauce with Mozzarella
Not-Really Pesto Sauce
Squid and Bacon Sauce
Wednesday Night Comfort Pasta
Mushroom and Chicory Sauce
Summer Tomato Sauce
Pasta with Olive Paste and Burnt Onions
Spaghetti with Two Cheeses
Ultra-Quick Fennel Sauce
Salsa Prezzemolo (Pungent Parsley Sauce)
Penne with Pimentos and Choriza
Penne with Pesto and Beans
Desperation Pasta

These dishes represent pasta at its fastest. All are designed to be prepared and cooked in no more time than it takes to boil water and cook the pasta – in other words, around 20 minutes from start to finish. Naturally, this means there are no fancy sauces in here. But that's not the purpose of the chapter. Its purpose is to show how you can eat really well on a Tuesday or Wednesday evening without either (A) going to a lot of trouble or (B) ordering a takeaway.

Because these are designed for midweek eating, when you're likely to be on your own or with the person you live with, the recipes are presented in quantities serving two people. But all are worth making just for yourself: simply cut the quantities in half. And all are worth making for four, when you're having friends over but don't want to do a lot of kitchen work. In that case, just double the quantities and you're ready to roll.

One word of explanation about the presentation of the recipes. Each of them begins with the words: 'Boil a large pot of water for the pasta and get it cooking.' After that follows the method for preparing and cooking the sauce. Please note that the action described by the first sentence of each recipe really describes *three* separate stages. *First:* put the water on to boil and then start going about the preparation and cooking described in the rest of the method. *Second:* when the water has come to a boil, salt it, put in the pasta, stir for 30 seconds to prevent sticking, then let it get on with cooking. *Third:* when you've put the pasta in and stirred, go back to finish off the rest of the preparation and cooking. If you remember these three stages, all these sauces can easily be cooked before the pasta is done.

Quasi Puttanesca Sauce

225g (8oz) pasta
5 anchovies
15ml (1tbsp) capers
1 large clove garlic
1 small red chilli
75ml (5tbsp) extra virgin olive oil

Boil a large pot of water for the pasta and get it cooking. Put the anchovies and capers in a strainer to drain them. Chop the garlic very fine and crumble or chop the chilli. Put the garlic and chilli in a small pan with 15ml (1tbsp) of the oil and cook over a gentle heat till they're sizzling lightly. Meanwhile, chop the drained anchovies and capers roughly. Add to the pan and cook for another two minutes. Turn off the heat.

When the pasta is done, add the remaining oil to the mixture in the pan. Drain the cooked pasta, and toss with the sauce.

THIS DISH NEEDS NO CHEESE.

Quick Tomato and Garlic Sauce

This delicious sauce can be varied in many ways; these are nothing more than the basics.

225g (8oz) pasta
2 cloves garlic
1 x 400g (14oz) tin plum tomatoes
15ml (1tbsp) vegetable oil
5ml (1tsp) dried mixed herbs, or a single herb
such as rosemary or thyme
30-45ml (2-3tbsp) extra virgin olive oil
freshly grated Parmesan for serving

Boil a large pot of water for the pasta and get it cooking. Meanwhile, peel the garlic and chop it fine or coarse, as you prefer. Open the tin of tomatoes so they're ready – they need to go into the pan at a moment's notice. Get the oil very hot in a nonstick frying pan and put in the garlic. Let it cook just for a few seconds, till it's sizzling, then add the herbs and the tomatoes; if the tomatoes are not chopped, chop them roughly with the edge of your spatula or wooden spoon. Season well with salt and pepper, and cook hard till the sauce is a thick sludge (around five-ten minutes). Turn off the heat and leave till the pasta's cooked.

Just before the pasta is done, reheat the sauce gently with the extra virgin olive oil. Pour over the cooked pasta and serve immediately.

To vary the recipe, add onions or a stalk of celery with the garlic. Splash in a little dry white wine or vermouth when cooking the sauce. Add a bit of chilli, tomato paste, or capers or olives. Anything you want to try will probably work just fine.

Quick Spinach and Garlic Sauce

Frozen spinach is incredibly useful for cooks in a hurry. Since spinach can happily absorb almost any quantity of garlic, you can use five or six cloves instead of two or three. You can also use cream instead of all or part of the extra virgin olive oil.

225g (8oz) pasta
2-3 cloves garlic
1 medium onion
5ml (1tsp) vegetable oil
450g (1lb) frozen chopped spinach
a small grating of nutmeg
60-75ml (4-5tbsp) extra virgin olive oil
freshly grated Parmesan for serving

Boil a large pot of water for the pasta and get it cooking. Meanwhile, finely chop the garlic and slice the onion very thin. Get the vegetable oil very hot in a large frying pan and throw in the garlic and onion. Stir for a minute or so, to colour the garlic and onion lightly, then add the spinach with a generous dose of salt and pepper. Cook, with regular stirring, till it's thoroughly defrosted and has lost most of its water content (around six-eight minutes). Add the nutmeg while it's cooking. Turn off the heat and let it sit till the pasta is nearly done. At the last minute, turn the heat back on and add the extra virgin olive oil. Heat through and toss with the pasta. Serve with grated Parmesan.

Smoked Salmon, Sour Cream and Chives

I think smoked salmon should never, ever, be cooked – as it sometimes is in pasta recipes. There's a good reason for trying, however: the combo is great. And when the salmon is just added at the end, as in this ultra-luxurious dish, it will show itself at its best.

225g (8oz) pasta
75ml (5tbsp) sour cream
225g (4oz) smoked salmon slices
(or cheaper off-cuts if you want to economise)
small handful chives

Boil a large pot of water for the pasta and get it cooking. Next, gently heat the sour cream in a small saucepan; it will just need a few minutes, to become hot but not boiling. Meanwhile, cut the salmon into thin shreds and the chives into small pieces. When the pasta is cooked, toss it with the cream, salmon and chives, and plenty of freshly ground black pepper. Serve immediately with a salad.

THIS DISH NEEDS NO CHEESE.

Caper Sauce

Ultra-light, zingy and simple. The sauce can also be used for a pasta salad, and is just as good with plainly cooked fish or chicken.

225g (8oz) pasta
15ml (1tbsp) capers
juice of 1 lime
1 small green or red pepper
10ml (2tsp) red wine vinegar
30-45ml (2-3tbsp) extra virgin olive oil

Boil a large pot of water for the pasta and get it cooking. Meanwhile, chop the capers, and de-seed and finely chop the pepper. Mix all ingredients and leave to blend while the pasta finishes cooking. Toss with the cooked, drained pasta and serve immediately.

THIS DISH NEEDS NO CHEESE.

Tomato, Lemon and Basil Sauce

There isn't much in this sauce, but what there is, is very pungent. Light and delicious.

225g (8oz) pasta
3 sun-dried tomatoes
75ml (5tbsp) extra virgin olive oil
½ a lemon
small handful fresh basil

Boil a large pot of water for the pasta and get it cooking. Finely chop the tomatoes and put them in a small pan with 15ml (1tbsp) of the oil. Heat gently for a few minutes, while you grate the zest from the lemon peel and then squeeze out the juice. Add the zest to the tomato and oil, and turn the heat off. Meanwhile, coarsely chop the basil or tear in small pieces with your hands. When the pasta is done, toss with the tomato mixture, the remaining oil, and the lemon juice. Top with the basil and serve immediately.

THIS DISH NEEDS NO CHEESE.

Sausage and Garlic Sauce

You can use almost any sausage for this, as long as it is a good one – preferably bought from a butcher – and not mass-produced. But I hope you never buy those sausages anyway!

225g (8oz) pasta
225g (8oz) good sausages
60-75ml (4-5tbsp) extra virgin olive oil
4-5 cloves garlic
45ml (3tbsp) dry white wine or vermouth
small handful fresh parsley
freshly grated Parmesan for serving

Boil a large pot of water for the pasta and get it cooking. Meanwhile, snip the sausages out of their skins and cut into chunks. Heat 15ml (1tbsp) of the oil in a large frying pan and fry the sausage pieces till they're browned all over (around 15 minutes). Meanwhile, chop the garlic finely. Add the garlic to the pan for the last few minutes of cooking along with the wine, and cook down till the wine is well reduced and the garlic lightly browned. You can chop the parsley in the meantime. Toss everything with the cooked pasta and serve with the cheese passed around separately.

Pasta with Garlic, Chilli and Peas

Frozen peas are another of the great larder standbys. Frozen broad beans could be used instead.

225g (8oz) pasta
1 clove of garlic
1 small dried red chilli, de-seeded
½ a small lemon
60ml (4tbsp) extra virgin olive oil
225g (8oz) frozen peas

Boil a large pot of water for the pasta and get it cooking. Meanwhile, finely chop the chilli and garlic; peel off a broad strip of lemon zest and cut into very fine shreds; and squeeze the juice from the lemon half. Heat 15ml (1tbsp) of the oil over a low heat in a small frying pan, and cook the garlic and chilli for 30 seconds or so. Add the lemon zest and peas with a little water (or wine, or stock), and cover the pan. Cook till the peas are done (around another five minutes). Turn off the heat and leave to sit.

When the pasta is cooked, drain it and put it in a bowl. Pour on the oil mixture plus the remaining oil, then add the lemon juice and toss well. This dish needs no Parmesan, but you could add fresh herbs if you have some.

THIS DISH NEEDS NO CHEESE.

Basic Cream Sauce

Cream has a bad name because it is — let's not mince words here — fattening stuff. But it also happens to be one of the perfect partners for pasta, and as long as you don't eat it too often you will not suffer the pains of weight-gain. This is a basic recipe followed by a few variations. All simple, all fast, and all *extremely* delicious.

225g (8oz) pasta
around 120ml (8tbsp) double cream
a hefty knob of butter
freshly grated Parmesan for serving

Boil a large pot of water for the pasta and get it cooking. Meanwhile, put the cream in a small saucepan with a little salt and pepper; bring to the boil, then turn down the heat a little and simmer for three-four minutes. Add the butter towards the end, as it only needs a few seconds of melting time. If you like, you can boil up half or two-thirds of the cream and add the remainder just before cooking.

The sauce can also be made in the microwave, and right in the serving bowl. Proceed exactly as in the recipe, but cook in thirty-second spurts at full power. The sauce should need no more than two minutes. Add butter at the end and let it melt in the heat of the cream.

Creamy Sun-dried Tomato Sauce

225g (8oz) pasta
2-3 sun-dried tomatoes in oil
a hefty knob of butter
around 120ml (8tbsp) double cream
freshly grated Parmesan for serving

Boil a large pot of water for the pasta and get it cooking. Finely chop the tomatoes, then put them with the butter in a small saucepan. Cook gently for a minute or two, then add the cream, bring to the boil, and turn down the heat a little to simmer for three-four minutes. If you like, you can boil up half or two-thirds of the cream and add the remainder just before cooking. The sauce can also be made in the microwave, using the procedure described in the preceding recipe.

Creamy Prosciutto Sauce

225g (8oz) pasta
150g (6oz) prosciutto
around 120ml (8tbsp) double cream
a hefty knob of butter
freshly grated Parmesan for serving

Boil a large pot of water for the pasta and get it cooking. Meanwhile, cut the prosciutto into thin shreds. Put the cream in a small saucepan, bring to the boil, then turn down the heat a little and simmer for three-four minutes. Stir in the prosciutto, just to heat through, then the butter. If you like, you can boil up half or two-thirds of the cream and add the remainder just before cooking.

Olive and Chilli Sauce

225g (8oz) pasta
100g (4oz) stoned green olives,
preferably a type that has some
additional flavour such as herbs, garlic or lemon
1 small green chilli
1 small green pepper
around 30ml (2tbsp) extra virgin olive oil
small handful fresh parsley, preferably the flat-leafed type
freshly grated Parmesan for serving

Boil a large pot of water for the pasta and get it cooking.
Meanwhile, chop the olives and peppers together to make a fairly
fine mixture. This can be done in a food processor in less time than
it takes to read this sentence. If you wish, you can heat them
quickly in a small saucepan or the microwave, but this really isn't
necessary.

When the pasta is cooked, drain it a little less thoroughly than
usual, as the sauce is on the dry side. Toss pasta and sauce in a bowl,
and eat it straight from there with freshly grated Parmesan.

Herb Sauce

The herb can be dill, basil, parsley, mint – anything that doesn't need cooking. Just use a generous amount, with lots of extra virgin olive oil. You can also use a combination of herbs if you wish.

225g (8oz) any pasta
1-2 cloves garlic, finely chopped
60-75ml (4-5tbsp) extra virgin olive oil
small handful fresh herbs
freshly grated Parmesan for serving

Boil a large pot of water for the pasta and get it cooking. Meanwhile, finely chop the garlic and warm the oil in a small, heavy saucepan or frying pan. Cook the garlic in the oil very gently while you chop the herbs (around two-three minutes). Turn off the heat and leave till the pasta is cooked. Drain it, mix the herbs into the garlic oil, and toss with the pasta. Pass the cheese around separately.

There is no end to the variations you can work with this simple dish. A sun-dried tomato or fresh chilli, finely chopped, can be cooked with the garlic. Butter can be substituted for all or part of the oil. One or two spring onions can be used instead of garlic.

Quick Tuna Sauce

This simple recipe is delicious just as it is, but it can easily (and happily) be perked up with other flavourings – capers, chillies, spring onions, herbs, the chopped zest from a strip of lemon peel. And it's a great last-minute meal when there's not much to eat in the house, since all the ingredients are larder standbys.

225g (8oz) pasta
1 x 150g (6oz) tin of tuna
1-2 cloves garlic
30ml (2tbsp) dry white wine or vermouth
45-60ml (3-4tbsp) extra virgin olive oil
freshly grated Parmesan for serving

Boil a large pot of water for the pasta and get it cooking. Meanwhile, drain the tuna well. Heat 15ml (1tbsp) of the oil in a frying pan and fry the garlic with some salt and pepper till it colours very lightly (around two minutes). Now add the tuna, flaking it lightly with a fork or spatula, and the wine. Cook just to heat through thoroughly and evaporate the wine. Turn off the heat, add the remaining oil, and leave till the pasta is done. Toss the drained, cooked pasta with the sauce, and serve with grated Parmesan.

Sun-dried Tomato Sauce With Mozzarella

Melting the mozzarella makes a gooey, stringy mess – which is absolutely irresistible.

225g (8oz) pasta
2-3 sun-dried tomatoes, or 15ml (1tbsp) tomato purée
1-2 cloves garlic
30ml (2tbsp) extra virgin olive oil
30ml (2tbsp) dry white wine or vermouth
1 packet Italian mozzarella
freshly grated Parmesan for serving

Boil a large pot of water for the pasta and get it cooking. Meanwhile, finely chop the tomatoes and garlic, and cook them gently in half the olive oil for two-three minutes. Add the wine and cook till it's almost all evaporated. Chop the mozzarella into small pieces.

When the pasta is done, drain well and return to the pot in which you cooked it. Put in the tomato/garlic mixture, the remaining oil, and the mozzarella. Toss well until the cheese is melted and stringy, then serve with extra grated Parmesan.

Not-Really Pesto Sauce

Pesto sauce (basil, pine nuts, garlic, oil and cheese) is one of the glories of Italian pasta cookery. Unfortunately, you need masses of fresh basil to make your own. And the ready-made varieties, though useful, are not always great. This sauce compromises by using the pesto ingredients in a different way: not quite as wonderful as the real thing, perhaps, but still pretty good.

225g (8oz) long pasta – spaghetti, linguini etc.
2-3 cloves garlic
45ml (3tbsp) extra virgin olive oil
15ml (1tbsp) pine nuts
small handful fresh basil leaves
freshly grated Parmesan

Boil a large pot of water for the pasta and get it cooking. Meanwhile, chop the garlic very finely and put in a small pan with the oil, and cook it over a very low heat just till it starts to sizzle a bit (around two minutes). Add the pine nuts and some salt and pepper, and cook, stirring constantly, till the pine nuts are lightly coloured (around two minutes more). Turn off the heat and leave till the pasta is cooked, and in the meantime tear the basil into small pieces. When the pasta is cooked, drain well and toss with the sauce and the basil. Add more extra virgin olive oil if it's too dry, and serve with lots of grated cheese.

Squid and Bacon Sauce

The serious speed in this recipe comes from buying squid in ready-prepared rings and the bacon in shreds (lardons). But preparing those items yourself will only add a few minutes' work, if you can't buy them pre-prepared. And the sauce is worth the extra work.

225g (8oz) pasta
a splash of extra virgin olive oil or a small knob of butter
100g (4oz) bacon shreds
1 medium onion
100g (4oz) squid, cut into rings
15ml (1tbsp) dry white wine or vermouth
a few sprigs of fresh thyme or sage,
or 2.5ml (1tsp) dried grated Parmesan for serving

Boil a large pot of water for the pasta and get it cooking. Put the bacon in a nonstick pan with the oil or butter (which helps get the fat running from the bacon more quickly). Turn on the heat and cook the bacon gently for a few minutes. Meanwhile, cut the onion in thick slices. Add the onion, turn up the heat, and stir-fry briskly until the onion and bacon are both lightly browned (around 3-4 minutes). Now add the squid, wine and herbs; season with salt and pepper, and continue cooking just until the squid is done (around 2-3 minutes). The heat may be turned off now if the pasta isn't done. When it is done, drain well and toss with the sauce. Serve immediately with the cheese passed separately.

Wednesday Night Comfort Pasta

Has your boyfriend cancelled dinner? Your boss ticked you off? Your mum given you grief for not going to visit last weekend? If the answer is yes to any of the above, make this dish. Utilising one of the great food combinations, bacon and onions, it derives its inspiration from spaghetti à la Carbonara, but it's even simpler than that – so simple I don't even like to call it a dish. All you need is a few rashers of bacon, a scrap of any cheese (even basic Cheddar), an onion and some pasta. A single bite will cheer you up. A whole plateful will have you singing along to The Spice Girls while you do the washing up.

225g (8oz) pasta
2-4 rashers bacon
1 medium onion
30ml (2tbsp) dry white wine or vermouth
a lump of any old cheese, as long as it's good

Boil a large pot of water for the pasta and get it cooking. Put the bacon in a nonstick pan, with a little oil or butter if it's very lean, and cook till it's done the way you like it. Meanwhile, chop the onion. When the bacon is cooked, remove to drain on kitchen towels while you fry the onion till lightly coloured in the bacon fat. Add the wine and cook down, scraping the pan to release all the delicious stuck-on bits. Grate the cheese. When the pasta is done, drain well, then put in the pan with the onion and toss well to coat with the pan juices. Turn out into two bowls, grate on lots of black pepper, and top with cheese. Take a bite. See, don't you feel better already?

Mushroom and Chicory Sauce

Rocket or watercress can be used instead of chicory in this dish, which is a cross between pasta and a salad.

225g (8oz) pasta
225g (8oz) mushrooms
30ml (2tbsp) extra virgin olive oil
1 head chicory
10ml (2tsp) balsamic vinegar
grated Parmesan to serve

Boil a large pot of water for the pasta and get it cooking. Wipe the mushrooms clean and slice thickly, and heat the oil over a moderate heat in a large frying pan. Put in the mushrooms, season with salt and pepper, and cook, stirring a few times, till they're barely done (around three minutes). Meanwhile, trim the chicory and slice thinly. When the pasta is done, drain well and toss with the mushrooms (plus all their oil), the chicory, and the vinegar. If the sauce seems dry, drizzle on a little more oil before serving with the grated cheese.

Summer Tomato Sauce

This can be made only when really good, ripe tomatoes are available – in other words, during the summer months. The tomatoes are given nothing more than a quick heating in olive oil, so they retain their summery freshness, and there's nothing more to it than garlic and basil. Incredibly simple and incredibly delicious.

225g (8oz) pasta
225g (8oz) red, ripe tomatoes
2-3 cloves garlic
60ml (4tbsp) extra virgin olive oil
large handful fresh basil or coriander
grated Parmesan for serving

Boil a large pot of water for the pasta and get it cooking. Meanwhile, core the tomatoes, halve them, and scoop out all the jelly and seeds. Put them in a sieve or colander to drain as you work. NB: If you want to peel the tomatoes first, prick each one with a sharp knife and put them in another pot of boiling water, one at a time, for a count of ten. Using a slotted spoon to hold them makes it easier to fish them out. Then peel and proceed with coring and removing jelly and seeds.

Finely chop the garlic and the herbs. Heat half the oil in a large frying pan and put in the garlic for a few seconds, just to let it sizzle briefly, then add the tomatoes, toss quickly, season with salt and pepper, and turn off the heat. When the pasta is cooked, drain well and toss with the tomatoes and herbs and the extra oil. Serve immediately with grated Parmesan.

Pasta With Olive Paste and Burnt Onions

This very easy recipe makes use of the olive pastes, both green and black, which are widely available from delicatessens and supermarkets. You could add a little bacon, if you have some, when frying the onions.

225g (8oz) pasta
1 medium onion
15ml (1tbsp) vegetable oil
30ml (2tbsp) olive paste
30ml (2tbsp) extra virgin olive oil
grated Parmesan for serving

Boil a large pot of water for the pasta and get it cooking. Meanwhile, slice the onion very thinly and heat the oil very hot in a nonstick frying pan. Put in the onion, season with salt and pepper, and stir-fry briskly till it is very soft and deeply browned – even blackened in spots is fine. This should take around five minutes. Turn off the heat and leave till needed. When the pasta is cooked, drain well and toss with the onion, olive paste, and olive oil. Serve the grated Parmesan separately.

Spaghetti with Two Cheeses

This is essentially spaghetti 'all'Inglese' – with butter and Parmesan. It's one of my favourite pasta dishes, and few are simpler. This version gains a little bit extra from the use of another cheese. If you don't have access to Gruyère, use a mature Cheddar or even Cheshire – anything with a decently tangy taste.

225g (8oz) spaghetti
50g (2oz) Gruyère
a very generous knob of butter
grated Parmesan for serving

Boil a large pot of water for the pasta and get it cooking. Grate the Gruyère and the Parmesan, if it isn't already grated. When the pasta is done, drain well and toss with the Gruyère, the butter, and a bit of Parmesan. Toss quickly, and add more butter if the pasta seems too dry. Serve immediately with the rest of the Parmesan and a green salad.

Ultra-Quick Fennel Sauce

If you like fennel as much as I do, you will love this dish. The same treatment can be used for almost any green veg, including courgettes and broccoli. For a slow version of fennel sauce, see page 61.

225g (8oz) short pasta, such as fusilli or penne
350g (12oz) fennel
45ml (3tbsp) extra virgin olive oil
30ml (2tbsp) dry white wine or vermouth
grated Parmesan for serving

Boil a large pot of water for the pasta and get it cooking. Snip the green frilly fronds from the fennel and set them aside; they will be used as a garnish. Now top and tail the bulbs and slice them thinly. Heat 15ml (1tbsp) of the oil over a high heat in a large, heavy frying pan and put in the fennel. Season with salt and pepper, and stir-fry briskly till the fennel is lightly softened and slightly charred or blistered in spots (around five-seven minutes). Add the stock and wine, let it bubble away, and turn off the heat till needed. The fennel can be cooked well in advance and left in its pan to cool, uncovered. Meanwhile, chop the fronds finely.

When the pasta is done, drain well and toss with the fennel, chopped fronds, and remaining oil. Serve immediately with lots of grated Parmesan.

Salsa Prezzemolo (Pungent Parsley Sauce)

This is adapted from a recipe in Patricia Wells's excellent book *Trattoria*. It also goes well with chicken or meat.

2 cloves garlic
3 anchovy fillets, well drained
large handful fresh parsley, preferably the flat-leafed type
20ml (4tsp) lemon juice
60ml (4tbsp) extra virgin olive oil

Boil a large pot of water for the pasta and get it cooking. Meanwhile, finely chop the garlic and anchovies with the salt; this is easiest in a food processor. Now coarsely chop the parsley and add it to the garlic/anchovy mixture, or just put in the food processor and pulse two or three times. The parsley should not be too fine, so that the sauce has a slightly coarse, chunky texture. Finally add the lemon juice and then the oil, pouring in a thin, steady stream. Season with black pepper and with salt if it's needed. When the pasta is done, drain well and toss with the sauce.

THIS DISH NEEDS NO CHEESE.

Penne with Pimentos and Chorizo

Chorizo is a delicious sausage from Spain, but its full flavour goes well with pasta. If you can't find a jar of peppers in oil, use fresh peppers and cook them for a few minutes longer.

500g (1lb 2oz) penne
3 peppers preserved in oil
2 cloves garlic
225g (8oz) Spanish chorizo sausage
45ml (3tbsp) extra virgin olive oil
small handful parsley
grated Parmesan for serving

Boil a large pot of water for the pasta and get it cooking. Meanwhile, cut the peppers in shreds around 5mm (¼in) wide, finely chop the garlic, and slice the sausage thinly. Heat 15ml (1tbsp) of the oil in a large frying pan, and cook the sausage for a minute or two, till some of the fat starts to run out. Add the peppers and garlic and cook, with frequent stirring, for a couple of minutes more. Season with black pepper but leave salt for later, as the sausage may be quite salty. Finely chop the parsley.

When the pasta is cooked, drain well and toss with the contents of the pan. Sprinkle on the parsley and serve with grated Parmesan.

Penne with Pesto and Beans

This is based on a Genoese dish. Needless to say, it will be much, much better if made with home-made pesto. Needless to say, pesto from a jar is easier.

225g (8oz) penne
225g (8oz) French beans
45ml (3tbsp) pesto sauce
grated Parmesan for serving

Boil a large pot of water for the pasta and get it cooking. At the same time, boil another pot of water for the beans. Meanwhile, top and tail the beans and rinse them well; you don't need to dry them. When their water is boiling hard, salt it well and put the beans in. Bring back to the boil, then cook for two-three minutes more, just long enough to cook them *al dente*. Drain off the water, and set aside. When the pasta is cooked, drain well and toss with the pesto and the beans. Season with salt and pepper, and serve immediately with the cheese.

Desperation Pasta

You know what it's like: you get home late and there's *nothing* to eat. And you're starving. This is the dish for those evenings. It assumes that you have just three things on hand: dried pasta, extra virgin olive oil and an onion. It is better if you have two other things: grated cheese (in your freezer, remember?) and a splash of dry white wine or vermouth. If you have those things – and I hope you always do – you can make this dead-simple dish in the time it takes to boil water and cook the pasta.

225g (8oz) pasta
1-2 medium onions
around 45ml (3tbsp) extra virgin olive oil
generous splash of dry white wine or vermouth (optional)
grated Parmesan for serving

Boil a large pot of water for the pasta and get it cooking. Meanwhile, halve the onion lengthwise and slice medium-thick; if you happen to have a clove of garlic, you can chop it and cook it with the onion.

Put a little of the oil in a nonstick frying pan and turn the heat on medium-high. Add the onion (and garlic if using), plus a generous dose of salt and pepper. Stir-fry briskly just till the onion starts to colour (1-2 minutes), then add the wine and cook down till the onions are soft but not squishy (3-4 minutes more). If not using the wine, turn the heat down after the onions have coloured and cook for 6-7 minutes more. Turn off the heat and leave in the pan if the sauce is done before the pasta.

Drain the pasta well and toss with the remaining olive oil. Add the onions, stir well, and serve immediately with the cheese.

Nice and Quick

Grilled Red Pepper and Tomato Sauce
Roasted Asparagus and Lemon Sauce
Pasta with Spicy Squid and Mushroom Sauce
Pasta with Garlic Sauce
Pasta with Garlic Cream Sauce
Pasta with Not-quite Carbonara Sauce
Tomato Sauce with Beans and Peas
Pasta with Smooth Broccoli Sauce
Cream Sauce with Bacon, Onions and Peas
Pasta with Mushroom Cream Sauce
Pasta with Courgette-Cream Sauce
Cauliflower and Fresh Tomato Sauce
Pasta with French Bean and Red Onion Sauce
Pasta with Tomato Sauce and Charred Onions
Pasta with Pan-Braised Fennel Sauce
Bucatini All 'Amatriciana
Pasta Picante with Grilled Peppers
Pasta with Tomato Sauce, Bacon and Olives
Pepper and Courgette Sauce
Spicy Aubergine Sauce
Fennel and Sausage Sauce
Penne with Aubergine and Tomato

These dishes are the in-between dishes – not very quick to cook, but they don't take ages either. They are designed for either a week night or a weekend party, and the emphasis is on speed even if it isn't on lightning speed. In most dishes, there is much less work involved than there is time. For instance, a dish like ROASTED ASPARAGUS AND LEMON SAUCE takes around 30 minutes from beginning to end, but most of that time is accounted for by preheating the oven and roasting the asparagus – neither of which requires much attention on your part. Thus, it only takes a little planning and preparation to fit the dishes into a busy working-day schedule. There's a heavy emphasis here on vegetables, because vegetables are particularly well suited to this type of sauce. But you can add a bit of meaty flavour to many of the vegetarian dishes through the use of bacon, prosciutto or ham.

Grilled Red Pepper and Tomato Sauce

500g (1lb 2oz) pasta
2 large red peppers
1 x 400g (14oz) tin plum tomatoes
1 bay leaf
2 cloves garlic
1 small onion
150g (6oz) green olives, pitted and roughly chopped
75ml (5tbsp) extra virgin olive oil
small handful parsley

Grill the peppers till the skin is blistered and lightly blackened all over – but not charred to a crisp, which makes them hard to peel. This should take around 15 minutes. Peel and chop into thin strips, then cut the strips in half and set aside.

Meanwhile, finely chop the garlic and onion and cook gently in 15ml (1tbsp) of the oil for a minute or two. Add the tomatoes and bay leaf, season with salt and pepper, and cook slowly for around 15 minutes, till the sauce is well reduced. Remove the bay leaf and put in the shredded peppers. Chop the parsley finely.

Bring plenty of water to a boil and cook the pasta. When it's a minute away from being ready, gently heat the tomato sauce (if necessary). Drain the cooked pasta, pour on the sauce, and top with minced parsley.

THIS DISH NEEDS NO CHEESE.

Roasted Asparagus and Lemon Sauce

This couldn't be simpler or more delicious.

500g (1lb 2oz) pasta
450g (1lb) asparagus
75ml (5tbsp) extra virgin olive oil
5ml (1tsp) coarse sea salt
juice and shredded zest of half a lemon

Boil a large pot of water for the pasta. Meanwhile, preheat the oven to 200°C (400°F, Gas Mark 6). Trim the ends off the asparagus, cut the spears into short lengths, and rinse under cold water. Put in a roasting tin with 15ml (1tbsp) of the oil plus a light sprinkling of salt, and cook near the top of the oven for 12-15 minutes, till it's done *al dente*. You can prepare the lemon in the meantime, and everything may be prepared in advance to this point.

Boil a large pot of water for the pasta and get it cooking. When it's done, drain well, toss with the remaining oil, top with the asparagus and the lemon juice and zest. Season with extra salt and lots of pepper. Cheese is optional.

Pasta with Spicy Squid and Mushroom Sauce

500g (1lb 2oz) pasta
450g (1lb) fresh squid, whole or in prepared rings
100g (4oz) shiitake or cultivated mushrooms
1 clove garlic
1 shallot
2 small dried chillies
60ml (4tbsp) extra virgin olive oil
5ml (1tsp) wine vinegar

Boil a large pot of water for the pasta. Clean the squid and cut into thin rings if necessary. Clean and slice the mushrooms around 5mm (¼in) thick. Chop the garlic, shallots and chilli as fine as you can get them.

Heat 15ml (1tbsp) of the oil in a large frying pan and gently cook the garlic, shallots and chilli for a minute or so. Add the squid and mushrooms and cook over a moderate heat till almost cooked (two-three minutes).

Boil a large pot of water for the pasta and get it cooking. When it's done, drain and mix with the sauce, the remaining oil, and the vinegar; toss it well, and add more oil or a knob of butter if you wish. Serve immediately; Parmesan is optional.

Pasta with Garlic Sauce

This sauce is intensely lemony, and may be made with less lemon juice if you prefer.

500g (1lb 2oz) pasta
1 whole head of garlic
juice of 1 small lemon
10ml (2tsp) tomato purée
around 80ml (3fl oz) extra virgin olive oil
a few sprigs or leaves of fresh herbs,
e.g. dill, fennel, basil, parsley
grated Parmesan for serving

Boil a small pot of salted water while you separate the garlic cloves. Add the cloves to the water, boil for five minutes, then drain off the water and re-fill the pot with fresh salted water. Bring to the boil and cook at a good simmer till the garlic is soft (around 20 minutes). Meanwhile, finely chop the herbs. Squeeze the pulp out of the garlic and mash with a fork or mortar and pestle, then whisk with the lemon and tomato purée, and finally with the oil. Season with salt and pepper, mix in the herbs, and serve or leave to stand for a while. Boil a large pot of water for the pasta and get it cooking. When it's done, toss with the sauce and sprinkle on a little cheese before serving.

This sauce keeps well, so you can make enough for multiple servings and keep the rest in the fridge.

Pasta with Garlic Cream Sauce

This sauce is similar to the preceding one but based on cream rather than oil. It is rich, comforting and delicious.

500g (1lb 2oz) pasta
1 whole head of garlic
80ml (3fl oz) double cream
80ml (3fl oz) dry white wine or vermouth
lots of grated Parmesan for serving

Boil a small pot of salted water while you separate the garlic cloves. Add the cloves to the water, boil for five minutes, then drain off the water and re-fill the pot with fresh salted water. Bring to the boil and cook at a good simmer till the garlic is soft (around 20 minutes). Squeeze the pulp out of the garlic and mash with a fork or mortar and pestle, then return to the pot with the cream and wine. Cook down hard till the mixture is reduced to a thick creaminess, seasoning with salt and pepper as it cooks. Boil a large pot of water for the pasta and get it cooking. When it's done, toss with the sauce and serve with the cheese.

Pasta with Not-quite Carbonara Sauce

Spaghetti à la Carbonara is one of the greatest pasta dishes, and one of the most popular. This version uses olive oil instead of eggs as the base, and it is just as good. The quantity of sauce given will suffice for anything from 225-450g (8oz-1lb) of pasta.

500g (1lb 2oz) pasta
175g (6oz) good bacon
175g (6oz) onions
large knob butter
60ml (4tbsp) dry white wine or vermouth
100ml (4fl oz) extra virgin olive oil
grated Parmesan for serving

Cut the rinds off bacon and cut into thin shreds. Halve the onions lengthwise, then cut into thin slices. Heat the butter in a medium frying pan and cook the bacon at a gentle pace until its fat starts to run. Add the onions and a good grinding of black pepper, and cook until onions are good and soft (around ten minutes). Add the wine, cook till it's boiled away, and spoon out some of the fat if you wish. May be prepared in advance to this point.

Boil a large pot of water for the pasta and get it cooking. When it's a few minutes from being done, reheat the bacon mixture and pour in the olive oil. Simmer gently for a couple of minutes at a very slow pace. Toss the sauce with the cooked, drained pasta in a big serving bowl, grind on more pepper, and serve immediately with freshly grated Parmesan.

Tomato Sauce with Beans and Peas

This is very hearty and very cheap — perfect for a winter dinner with friends.

1 x 400g (14oz) tin cannelini beans
1 clove garlic
1 dried red chilli
225g (8oz) small leeks, white part only
30ml (2tbsp) extra virgin olive oil
5ml (1tsp) dried oregano or tarragon or mixed herbs
225ml (8fl oz) tomato sauce
500g (1lb 2oz) short pasta

Rinse the beans under cold water and leave to drain. Meanwhile, finely chop the garlic and chilli, and cut the leeks into thin discs; put them in a sieve, run under cold water to clean, and shake the sieve to drain excess water. Heat the oil in a frying pan and cook the garlic for two-three minutes, taking care not to brown it, then add the herbs, beans and leeks. Season with salt and pepper, add the wine, and cook until the leeks are barely done (around ten minutes). Now add the tomato sauce and cook for another five minutes or so. May be prepared in advance to this point.

Boil a large pot of water for the pasta and get it cooking. When it's done, toss with the sauce and serve immediately with a green salad.

THIS DISH NEEDS NO CHEESE.

Pasta with Smooth Broccoli Sauce

This also goes well with potatoes or meat.

500g (1lb 2oz) pasta
225g (8oz) broccoli
100ml (4fl oz) chicken or vegetable stock
½ a green chilli, de-seeded
small handful fresh coriander, leaves and thin stems
15-30ml (1-2tbsp) double cream
grated Parmesan for serving

Separate the broccoli stalks from the florets, and peel the stalks. Cook them – either by steaming or by boiling in plenty of well salted water – till soft. This will take around five minutes in water, ten minutes in the steamer.

Put the stock in your blender, get the motor running, and add the chilli and broccoli a few pieces at a time. Purée till smooth, then add the cream and coriander, and blend just long enough to mix well. May be prepared in advance to this point.

Boil a large pot of water for the pasta and get it cooking. When it's done, toss with the sauce and serve with lots of grated Parmesan and black pepper.

Cream Sauce with Bacon, Onions and Peas

500g (1lb 2oz) pasta
125-175g (4-6oz) bacon
1 smallish onion, around 125g (4oz)
a 125g (4oz) bag of frozen peas
small splash of dry white wine or vermouth
around 120ml (8tbsp) double cream
a hefty knob of butter
plenty of freshly grated Parmesan for serving

Cut the rinds off the bacon and cut it into thin shreds. Put it in a heavy frying pan or saucepan, and bring to a sizzle over a fairly high heat. Stir once. Slice the onion and add to the pan. Run the peas under cold water to remove any ice and separate them. Season the bacon and onion with black pepper, then add the peas and the wine with a small splash of water. Cook, stirring occasionally, till the peas are just about done (around two-three minutes more). Then add the cream and butter, and cook down for a minute or so. Add the butter, then turn off the heat. Boil a large pot of water for the pasta and get it cooking. When it's ready, toss with the sauce and serve with the cheese.

Pasta with Mushroom Cream Sauce

This is a mycophile's delight, especially if made with wild, shiitake, or chestnut mushrooms. It's substantial enough to serve as a main course.

450g (1lb) mushrooms
good knob unsalted butter
1 small green chilli
1 clove garlic
30ml (2tbsp) dry white wine or vermouth
80-100ml (3-4fl oz) double cream
small handful fresh parsley, preferably the flat-leafed type
grated Parmesan for serving

Slice the mushrooms around 5mm (¼in) thick. De-seed the chilli and chop it finely with the garlic. While you're heating the water, prepare the mushrooms. Melt the butter in a large, heavy pan and get the mushrooms cooking in it while you prepare the garlic and chilli (if using). Add to the pan, season with salt and pepper, and cook, stirring regularly, just till the mushrooms turn *al dente* (around five minutes). Add the wine and let it cook down to nothing, then pour in the cream and cook for one minute. While it's cooking, finely chop the parsley. May be prepared in advance to this point.

Boil a large pot of water for the pasta and get it cooking. The sauce should be reheated gently if necessary just before serving, and poured over the cooked pasta. Sprinkle on the parsley, toss well, and serve with grated Parmesan.

Pasta with Courgette-Cream Sauce

This is a full meal, since the large quantity of courgettes provides vegetables as well as sauce. The sauce will be fairly dry, however, so you can add more cream if you wish.

500g (1lb 2oz) pasta
675g (1lb 8oz) small courgettes
10ml (2tsp) vegetable oil, or a comparable quantity of butter
30-45ml (2-3tbsp) double cream or crème fraîche
very small handful fresh parsley, preferably the flat-leafed type,
or basil if you have some

While the pasta water is coming to the boil, thinly slice the courgettes and put them, with the oil/butter, in a large frying pan. Season with salt and pepper and cook, stirring every minute or so, till the courgettes are just done (around five-ten minutes). Add the cream, sprinkle on the herbs, and serve immediately over the cooked, drained pasta.

THIS DISH NEEDS NO CHEESE.

Cauliflower and Fresh Tomato Sauce

This is a sauce to make in summer, when the tomatoes are more likely to have a full flavour.

500g (1lb 2oz) pasta
1 medium cauliflower
450g (1lb) tomatoes
60-75ml (4-5tbsp) extra virgin olive oil
small handful parsley
grated Parmesan

Boil a large pot of water for the pasta and get it cooking. Meanwhile, get water boiling in a steamer. Cut the cauliflower into bite-sized pieces and steam till done (six-ten minutes). Halve the tomatoes and de-seed, then cut in thickish shreds; chop the parsley finely. Mix the cooked cauliflower with the tomatoes and oil, then toss with pasta and parsley. Serve with grated Parmesan.

Pasta with French Bean and Red Onion Sauce

This is like a stir-fry that's been turned into a sauce. It is also good on its own.

500g (1lb 2oz) short pasta
400g (14 oz) French beans
5ml (1tsp) vegetable oil
1 medium red onion
45ml (3tbsp) dry white wine or vermouth
45-60ml (3-4tbsp) extra virgin olive oil
grated Parmesan for serving

Top and tail the beans, cut them in half, and wash under cold water. Heat the vegetable oil in a large frying pan over a high heat, then tip in the beans. Season with salt and pepper and fry briskly, stirring frequently, till the beans are lightly coloured (around five minutes). Meanwhile, halve the onion lengthwise and slice thinly. When the beans have coloured, turn the heat down and put in a splash of water to cool the pan more quickly. When the water has evaporated, add the onion and stir-fry for a minute or two, then add the wine and continue cooking till the beans are cooked *al dente*. The mixture can be left if necessary, with the heat turned off, for 15-30 minutes at this point.

Boil a large pot of water for the pasta and get it cooking. Reheat the sauce gently with the extra virgin olive oil. Pour over the drained pasta and serve immediately with grated Parmesan.

Pasta with Tomato Sauce and Charred Onions

500g (1lb 2oz) pasta
1 x 400g (14oz) tin plum tomatoes
2 sun-dried tomatoes (in oil)
2 cloves garlic
2 medium onions
45-60ml (3-4tbsp) extra virgin olive oil
1 small dried red chilli, de-seeded
tiny pinch of oregano
tiny pinch of thyme
5ml (1tsp) tomato purée
15ml (1tbsp) dry white wine or vermouth
grated Parmesan (optional)

De-seed the tomatoes, chop coarsely, and drain. Chop the sun-dried tomatoes, garlic and chilli finely, and the onion in long shreds. Heat 15ml (1tbsp) of the oil medium-hot in a small frying pan and fry the sun-dried tomatoes, chilli, garlic and herbs for 30 seconds. Mix in tomatoes, wine and tomato purée, and cook for another minute. Remove to a bowl and wipe out the pan. May be prepared in advance to this point.

Boil a large pot of water for the pasta and get it cooking. When it's three-four minutes from done, heat the remaining oil very hot in the frying pan. Chop onion and fry till partially blackened (around three minutes). When the pasta is done, drain it and toss with the tomatoes and onions. Parmesan is optional for this recipe.

Pasta with Pan-Braised Fennel Sauce

I adore fennel. It is one of the vegetables I will always buy, when I see it, and would happily eat it three or four times a week. Though delicious raw it is even better cooked, and this treatment makes a fine sauce for pasta – or a side dish for chicken or meat, as it happens.

500g (1lb 2oz) pasta
675g (1lb 8ozs) fennel
225ml (8fl oz) chicken stock
30ml (2tbsp) dry white wine or vermouth
salt and pepper
500g (1lb 2oz) short pasta such as fusilli or penne
grated Parmesan for serving

Boil a large pot of water for the pasta but don't get it cooking yet. First of all, snip the green frilly fronds from the fennel and set them aside; they will be used as a garnish. Now top and tail the bulbs and slice them thinly. Heat 15ml (1tbsp) of the oil in a large, heavy frying pan and put in the fennel. Season with salt and pepper, and cook at a fairly brisk heat for a few minutes. Now add the stock and wine, and turn down the heat to medium, and cover the pan. Cook for around 20 minutes, stirring regularly, to get the fennel soft but with a bit of *al dente* bite. Towards the end of cooking, remove the lid so the stock can boil down to a few spoonfuls. Meanwhile, chop the fronds finely. The fennel can be cooked well in advance and left in its pan to cool, uncovered.

Cook the pasta, drain well, and toss with the fennel, the chopped fronds, and the remaining oil. Serve immediately with lots of grated Parmesan.

Bucatini All'Amatriciana

Bucatini is something like a hollow spaghetti, and it's the classic shape for this simple, spicy, totally wonderful Roman sauce. But another shape will do just fine if you can't get bucatini. Reduce the quantity of chilli if you don't like very spicy food.

500g (1lb 2oz) pasta
150g (6oz) streaky bacon
2-3 cloves garlic
2 dried red chillies
1 x 400g (1oz) tin tomatoes
15ml (1tbsp) extra virgin olive oil
grated Parmesan for serving

Cut the rinds off the bacon and slice it into matchstick-sized shreds. Put it in a frying pan over a medium heat and cook it, stirring regularly, until the fat starts to run (around five-ten minutes). Meanwhile, peel and chop the garlic, and de-seed and crumble the chillies; wash your hands after handling the chillies. Remove with a slotted spoon, to leave as much bacon fat in the pan as possible, then put in the garlic and chilli and stir-fry over a medium heat just long enough to make the garlic smell fragrant (around two-three minutes). Season with salt and pepper, then put in the tomatoes and bacon with a good grinding of black pepper, and continue cooking just long enough to reduce the tomatoes to a thick sludge.

Meanwhile, boil a large pot of water for the pasta and get it cooking. When it's done, drain well and toss with the sauce plus the olive oil. Serve with grated Parmesan and a green salad.

Pasta Picante with Grilled Peppers

This takes hardly any time as long as you have some tomato sauce to hand. If you don't have home-made, something good from a jar will do. And the sauce can be cooked well in advance for last-minute reheating.

500g (1lb 2oz) pasta
2 large red peppers
225ml (8fl oz) tomato sauce (see page 34)
3-4 spring onions
1 fresh green chilli
large knob butter
150g (6oz) green olives, pitted and roughly chopped
30ml (2tbsp) capers, roughly chopped
30ml (2tbsp) extra virgin olive oil
small handful parsley

Grill the peppers till the skin is blackened. Peel and chop into thin strips, then cut the strips in half and set aside. Meanwhile, chop the spring onions and chilli very finely (de-seeding the chilli first if you want to take some of the heat out). Melt the butter in a frying pan or saucepan, and cook the onion and chilli over a low heat for two-three minutes.

Boil a large pot of water for the pasta and get it cooking. Add the tomato sauce to the onion and chilli, cook gently for five minutes, then add the olives and capers. Cook gently for a few minutes more, then turn off the heat and add the oil. All these stages may be completed well in advance.

When the pasta is nearly done, finely chop the parsley. Mix the sauce with the drained pasta, top with the peppers, and sprinkle on the parsley.

THIS DISH NEEDS NO CHEESE.

Pasta with Tomato Sauce, Bacon and Olives

The ideal bacon is Italian pancetta, but ordinary British-style bacon can be used with excellent results. If you don't eat meat, omit the bacon and use double the quantity of onion and garlic.

500g (1lb 2oz) pasta
125g (4oz) pancetta or bacon
1 medium or large onion
1 clove garlic
1 dried or fresh red chilli
5ml (1tsp) herbes de Provence
1 x 400g (14oz)tin chopped plum tomatoes
small handful stoned green olives
45ml (3tbsp) extra virgin olive oil
grated Parmesan for serving

Boil a large pot of water for the pasta and get it cooking. Meanwhile, prepare the bacon and get it cooking gently in a large, heavy frying pan till its fat starts to run (around two-four minutes). Add the onion, garlic and chilli with the dried herbs and a good grinding of black pepper. Stir well and leave to cook for two-three minutes, stirring a few times, then add the tomatoes and cook for another few minutes. Meanwhile, coarsely chop the olives. Add the olives to the pan and stir in, then turn off the heat and add the olive oil. When the pasta is done, drain well and toss with the sauce. Serve with cheese passed around separately.

Pepper and Courgette Sauce

The abundant quantity of vegetable matter means that you can serve this as a one-dish meal for two people. If you wish, however, you can use it with a full 500g (1lb 2oz) packet of pasta to serve four diners, and eat a salad afterwards to complete the meal. If you don't eat meat, the bacon can be omitted and the onions fried in 15ml (1tbsp) extra virgin olive oil.

500g (1lb 2oz) pasta
100g (4oz) bacon, rinds removed if necessary
1 medium onion, thinly sliced
5ml (1tsp) vegetable oil
4 medium courgettes
2-3 red peppers
15ml (1tbsp) dry white wine or vermouth
45-60ml (3-4tbsp) extra virgin olive oil
small handful fresh basil, roughly torn or chopped
grated Parmesan for serving

Cut the bacon into thin shreds and put it in a large, heavy frying pan with the oil. Get them cooking at a fairly energetic pace while you slice the onion, and then put that in. Stir a few times while seasoning with salt and pepper. Prepare the courgettes and peppers by cutting the courgettes into thin discs and the peppers into shreds around 5mm (¼in) thick and 2.5cm (1in) long, then add them to the pan and cook till they're barely softened (around five minutes). Add the wine and let it cook down completely. Add the olive oil, and turn the heat down as far as it will go (or turn it off completely). The sauce is basically done, but can be left for a good while with the heat off if this suits your schedule.

Boil a large pot of water for the pasta and get it cooking. Meanwhile, reheat the sauce gently and pour it over the pasta. Stir in the basil and serve immediately with grated Parmesan. You could add a dash of chilli sauce somewhere along the line here, or a small chopped chilli with the bacon and onions.

Spicy Aubergine Sauce

500g (1lb 2oz) pasta
2 large aubergines, around 225-300g (8-10oz) each
2-3 cloves garlic
1 fresh red chilli
75-90ml (5-6tbsp) extra virgin olive oil
1 medium red onion
15ml (1tbsp) red wine vinegar
grated Parmesan for serving

Wash and dry the aubergines but do not do anything else with them. Thinly slice the garlic and crumble the chilli. Put the aubergines, garlic and chilli in a big, heavy frying pan that has a lid. Add 15ml (1tbsp) of the oil and bring to a gentle sizzle over a low heat. Season with salt and pepper, stir well, and cover the pan. Cook, turning the aubergines occasionally, until the aubergines are soft. This can take anything from 20-30 minutes, and may be done well in advance. When they're cooked, halve lengthwise, scoop out the soft flesh, and return it to the pan. (You will have to handle the aubergines carefully if they're still hot.)

Boil a large pot of water for the pasta and get it cooking. Thinly slice the onion and add to the pan with the aubergines. When the pasta is a few minutes away from being done, heat the sauce gently with the onion, vinegar and remaining olive oil. Just before serving, add the remaining oil and heat through. Serve with grated Parmesan.

Fennel and Sausage Sauce

You can use just about any good sausage for this; the Greek 'louganika' or Italian cooking sausages are particularly suitable. If you can't get fennel, use extra onion.

500g (1lb 2oz) pasta
2 medium heads of fennel
1 small onion
45ml (3tbsp) extra virgin olive oil
300g (10oz) sausage
1 x 400g (14oz) tin plum tomatoes
45ml (3tbsp) dry white wine or vermouth
grated Parmesan for serving

Chop the fennel and onion into bite-size pieces. Heat 15ml (1tbsp) oil over a medium heat in a large frying pan and add the fennel and onion with a good dose of salt and pepper. Cook, stirring occasionally, till they're slightly softened (three-four minutes). Meanwhile, cut the sausage into bite-size pieces. Add to the pan and continue cooking for another few minutes to colour the sausages slightly, then add the tomatoes and wine. Break up the tomatoes (if they're not already in pieces) and continue cooking for another ten-fifteen minutes, till the tomatoes are reduced to a thick sludge. May be prepared in advance to this point.

When you're ready to cook, boil a large pot of water for the pasta and get it cooking. When it's done, drain and toss with the sauce. Serve with grated Parmesan.

Penne with Aubergine and Tomato

This could also be served as a party dish, because the sauce is easy to prepare and cook in advance, but making it for larger numbers will require two frying pans. Use fresh tomatoes only if they are really red and ripe.

2 cloves garlic
around 80ml (3floz) extra virgin olive oil
1 small aubergine, around 250g (9oz) in weight
a few sprigs fresh rosemary, or 5ml (1tsp) dried
225g (8oz) fresh tomatoes, or 200g (7oz) tin tomatoes
225g (8oz) penne (or fusilli if you prefer)
grated Parmesan for serving

Boil a large pot of water for the pasta but don't get it cooking yet. Peel the garlic and slice it very thinly. Heat the oil in a large nonstick frying pan, and cook the garlic over a medium heat just until it colours very lightly (around 1 minute). Remove with a slotted spoon and set aside. Turn off the heat while you cut the aubergines into slices around 1.5cm thick. Turn the heat back on under the frying pan and, when it is medium-hot, quickly put in the aubergines. As soon as they are all in, turn them over; this method ensures that the oil gets taken up by both sides of the slices and lets you cook without adding more oil. Cook until they are well browned on one side (around 5-7 minutes), then turn and cook till soft all the way through and brown on the other side (another 5-6 minutes more). Once you've turned the slices, you can get the pasta cooking.

Meanwhile, core the tomatoes and cut into thick slices or wedges; if using tinned, drain them and coarsely chop.

When the aubergines are cooked, turn off the heat. Take a pair of clean scissors or kitchen shears and cut each slice into 3-4 pieces. Alternatively, you can remove them from the pan and cut slices with a knife. Return to the pan, add the tomatoes, rosemary and garlic, and cook for another minute or so – just long enough to heat the tomatoes through. Toss with the cooked, drained pasta, and serve immediately with the grated cheese.

Pasta Salads

Pasta Salad with Red Onion and Avocado
Pasta Salad with Cebollas en Escabeche
Pasta Salad with Salsa Cruda Mexicana
Pasta Salad with Scallops and Mange-Touts
Pasta Salad with Artichoke Hearts
Pasta Salad with Prawns and Prosciutto
Pasta Salad 'Niçoise'
Macaroni Salad
Pasta Salad with Marinated Salmon
Pink Pasta Salad
Pasta Salad with Herbed Crème Fraîche
Pasta Salad with Ginger, Carrots and Tomatoes
Pasta Salad with Tomato, Mozzarella and Basil
Ratatouille Pasta Salad

Pasta salads can be delicious, as long as you take certain precautions in preparing the pasta itself. This is because overcooked pasta is yukky, but overcooked pasta salad is disgusting. Overcooking must be avoided at all costs.

And it's easy to avoid if you follow the basic procedure outlined here. I've included it in each recipe as well, but read through once before proceeding to the recipes. Once you've got the basics down, you can enjoy some of the best and easiest pasta dishes around.

Cook the pasta in the usual way, then drain in a colander and run it under cold water to stop cooking. Drain it really well, shaking the colander hard to remove every last drop of water. Now turn it out onto a large, flat dish which will hold the pasta in something like a single layer, and toss gently with a little bit of oil. This will help keep the pasta from sticking together if it's to be left for a while. Do not refrigerate but try to use within an hour or so of cooking. It is then ready for any of the treatments following.

Pasta Salad with Red Onion and Avocado

This is also good with chicken or fish.

500g (1lb 2oz) short pasta such as fusilli or penne
2 small red onions, coarsely chopped
2 small green peppers, finely chopped
2.5ml (½tsp) ground cumin
2.5ml (½tsp) ground coriander
large pinch of cayenne
45ml (3tbsp) red wine vinegar
1-2 ripe avocados, depending on their size
30-45ml (2-3tbsp) extra virgin olive oil

Cook the pasta in the usual way, then drain in a colander and run it under cold water to stop cooking. Drain it really well, shaking the colander hard to remove every last drop of water. Now turn it out onto a large, flat dish which will hold the pasta in something like a single layer, and toss gently with a little bit of oil. This will help keep the pasta from sticking together if it's to be left for a while. Do not refrigerate but try to use within an hour or so of cooking.

Thinly slice the onions. De-seed the peppers, then slice them thinly as well and add to the onions in a glass or ceramic bowl. Add all remaining ingredients except the avocados and extra virgin olive oil, then leave for at least 1½ hours so the flavours can blend. Just before serving, peel and stone the avocados, and chop them around the same size as the onions. Mix in with the oil, taste for salt and pepper, and toss with the cooked pasta. Serve immediately with bread on the side and perhaps a bowl of olives.

Pasta Salad with Cebollas en Escabeche

This is something like a salsa, but it calls for long marinating and therefore must be made well in advance of the pasta. Your guests will gasp initially at the chilli-heat, but the 'burn' shouldn't last long. The sauce can also be eaten with any meat or poultry dish.

2 green chillies, preferable Anaheims, seeded and finely chopped
2 cloves garlic, thinly sliced
2 medium red onions, thinly sliced
1 bay leaf
60ml (4tbsp) red wine vinegar
30ml (2tbsp) extra virgin olive oil
2.5ml (½tsp) black peppercorns, coarsely crushed
2.5ml (½tsp) salt
2.5ml (½tsp) dried oregano
500g (1lb 2oz) short pasta, such as fusilli or penne

De-seed the chillies and chop them finely. Thinly slice the onion and garlic. Combine all ingredients in a glass or ceramic bowl and stir well. Cover and refrigerate at least 12 hours, and up to 48, stirring whenever you remember. Remove the bay leaf before serving.

Cook the pasta in the usual way, then drain in a colander and run it under cold water to stop cooking. Drain it really well, shaking the colander hard to remove every last drop of water. Now turn it out onto a large, flat dish which will hold the pasta in something like a single layer, and toss gently with a little bit of oil. This will help keep the pasta from sticking together if it's to be left for a while. Do not refrigerate but try to use within an hour or so of cooking.

Toss with the cooked, drained and cooled pasta, and serve immediately.

Pasta Salad with Salsa Cruda Mexicana

This simple relish is a staple of Mexican cooking but can easily and happily be adapted for use with pasta. Vary the chilli according to taste.

1 beef tomato, seeded and diced
1-2 fresh green chillies, seeded and finely chopped
1 small onion, finely chopped
small handful fresh coriander, coarsely chopped
1 clove garlic, finely chopped
15ml (1tbsp) red wine vinegar or lime juice
60ml (4tbsp) extra virgin olive oil
500g (1lb 2oz) short pasta, such as fusilli or penne

Cook the pasta in the usual way, then drain in a colander and run it under cold water to stop cooking. Drain it really well, shaking the colander hard to remove every last drop of water. Now turn it out onto a large, flat dish which will hold the pasta in something like a single layer, and toss gently with a little bit of oil. This will help keep the pasta from sticking together if it's to be left for a while. Do not refrigerate but try to use within an hour or so of cooking.

Mix all ingredients and season with salt to taste. Leave for 30 minutes so the flavours can blend, then toss with the cooked, drained, cooled pasta. Drizzle on the olive oil and serve immediately

Pasta Salad with Scallops and Mange-Touts

Use monkfish if you can't find scallops. This expensive, very special treat will serve four-six people as a main course.

225g (8 oz) mange-touts
2 large carrots
450g (1lb) scallops
60ml (4tbsp) extra virgin olive oil
7.5ml (½tbsp) red wine vinegar
7.5ml (½tbsp) lemon juice
2-3 spring onions
500g (1lb 2oz) short pasta, such as fusilli or penne

Bring two pots of salted water to the boil, one for the veg and one for the pasta. While waiting for them to boil, top and tail the mange-touts. Peel the carrots, then slice into thin discs. Blanch the mange-touts in a pot of rapidly boiling water till just done *al dente* (around one-two minutes), then remove with a slotted spoon and refresh under the cold tap. Drain well and set aside. Now add the carrots to the same pot and cook till just done *al dente* (around three-four minutes). Refresh, drain, and set aside.

Cook the pasta in the usual way, then drain in a colander and run it under cold water to stop cooking. Drain it really well, shaking the colander hard to remove every last drop of water. Now turn it out onto a large, flat dish which will hold the pasta in something like a single layer, and toss gently with a little bit of oil. This will help keep the pasta from sticking together if it's to be left for a while. Do not refrigerate but try to use within an hour or so of cooking.

Cook the scallops by steaming in a bowl (to catch the delicious juices) or by microwaving (covered) for three-four minutes. If microwaving, stir well a couple of times. Spread out on a large plate to cool, and strain the juices into a small bowl. When the juices are cool, mix with the oil and vinegar to make a vinaigrette. You can flavour it with a little garlic and mustard if you wish.

Pat the carrots and mange-touts dry and gently toss in a bowl with the vinaigrette. When the pasta is completely cool, put it in your serving bowl or platter, top with the scallops, and spread on the vegetables with their vinaigrette. Season with salt and pepper, and serve immediately.

Pasta Salad with Artichoke Hearts

Artichoke hearts are one of the best all-purpose larder standbys. This is also good with plainly cooked fish or chicken, and if you have peppers in a jar you can use those instead of fresh.

1 medium red onion, coarsely chopped
juice of 1 lime
2 green peppers
2 red peppers
8 artichoke hearts in oil, jarred not tinned
10ml (2tsp) red wine vinegar
45-60ml (3-4tbsp) extra virgin olive oil
500g (1lb 2oz) short pasta, such as fusilli or penne

Cook the pasta in the usual way, then drain in a colander and run it under cold water to stop cooking. Drain it really well, shaking the colander hard to remove every last drop of water. Now turn it out onto a large, flat dish which will hold the pasta in something like a single layer, and toss gently with a little bit of oil. This will help keep the pasta from sticking together if it's to be left for a while. Do not refrigerate but try to use within an hour or so of cooking.

Meanwhile, coarsely chop the onion, then mix it with the lime juice, season with salt and pepper, and leave to let flavours blend for at least ten minutes. Coarsely chop the peppers and artichoke hearts, and mix with the vinegar. Add to the cooked, cooled pasta and toss with the oil, using more as needed to make the dressing nice and oily. Serve immediately.

Pasta Salad with Prawns and Prosciutto

If pimentos are unavailable use grilled, peeled red peppers.

500g (1lb 2oz) short pasta, such as fusilli or penne
450g (1lb) cooked prawns
100g (4oz) smoked ham or prosciutto
4 red peppers in oil
1 medium red onion
3 small bulbs of fennel
60ml (4tbsp) extra virgin olive oil
5ml (1tsp) lemon juice
5ml (1tsp) sherry vinegar

Cook the pasta in the usual way, then drain in a colander and run it under cold water to stop cooking. Drain it really well, shaking the colander hard to remove every last drop of water. Now turn it out onto a large, flat dish which will hold the pasta in something like a single layer, and toss gently with a little bit of oil. This will help keep the pasta from sticking together if it's to be left for a while. Do not refrigerate but try to use within an hour or so of cooking.

Peel the prawns and halve lengthwise. Cover tightly and refrigerate till needed. Drain the pimentos and cut them, with the ham and onions, into thin shreds. Trim the fennel, removing the woody core, and slice into thin rings. Make a vinaigrette using half the olive oil, the lemon juice, and the vinegar plus a good grinding of pepper and a little salt. You can also add some chopped herbs if you have some on hand.

When you're ready to serve, toss the pasta with the prawns and pour on the dressing. Serve immediately.

Pasta Salad 'Niçoise'

This delicious dish takes its inspiration from the classic ingredients of the great Salade Niçoise of Provence. It's a meal in itself.

500g (1lb 2oz) short pasta, such as fusilli or penne
2 x 150g (6oz) tins tuna in oil
225g (8oz) black olives, or green if you prefer
4 hard-boiled eggs
1 small red onion
4 spring onions
8-10 leaves Cos lettuce
100ml (4fl oz) vinaigrette made with extra virgin olive oil

Cook the pasta in the usual way, then drain in a colander and run it under cold water to stop cooking. Drain it really well, shaking the colander hard to remove every last drop of water. Now turn it out onto a large, flat dish which will hold the pasta in something like a single layer, and toss gently with a little bit of oil. This will help keep the pasta from sticking together if it's to be left for a while. Do not refrigerate but try to use within an hour or so of cooking.

Drain the tuna well of oil, then flake it with a fork. Cut the olives in half if you wish, quarter the eggs, and cut the red onion and spring onions into thin shreds. Wash the lettuce and tear into large pieces.

Arrange the lettuce round the rim of your serving platter with the pasta heaped in the centre. Arrange all remaining ingredients over it, then drizzle on the vinaigrette as evenly as possible. Serve immediately with extra vinaigrette for those who want it, and with crusty French bread.

Macaroni Salad

This dish is a cliché of middle-American cooking – the sort of thing your grandma might make, or which you might be served at a church picnic. Despite that image, however, it can be one of the most delicious things imaginable – and perfect fare for a picnic or barbecue. If you don't make your own mayonnaise, use Hellmann's.

500g (1lb 2oz) elbow macaroni
1-2 red peppers
1-2 green peppers
2-3 stalks celery
5ml (1tsp) caraway or fennel seeds
5ml (1tsp) paprika
100ml (4fl oz) mayonnaise
45ml (3tbsp) sour cream (optional)
30ml (2tbsp) red wine vinegar

Cook the pasta in the usual way, then drain in a colander and run it under cold water to stop cooking. Drain it really well, shaking the colander hard to remove every last drop of water. Now turn it out onto a large, flat dish which will hold the pasta in something like a single layer, and toss gently with a little bit of oil. This will help keep the pasta from sticking together if it's to be left for a while. Do not refrigerate but try to use within an hour or so of cooking.

Meanwhile, de-seed the peppers and chop into fine dice, then top and tail the celery and chop in the same way. Mix all remaining ingredients to make the dressing, and season with salt and pepper.

When the pasta has cooled, toss well with the dressing. If possible, leave for 20 minutes or so before serving, to let the flavours blend.

Pasta Salad with Gazpacho Sauce

This is unorthodox but delicious.

500g (1lb 2oz) short pasta, such as fusilli or penne
450g (1lb) red, ripe tomatoes
20cm (8in) length of cucumber
1 red and 1 green pepper
100g (4oz) olives, green or black, stoned
1 small onion
1 clove garlic
2.5ml (½tsp) each of fennel, cumin and coriander seeds
100ml (4fl oz) extra virgin olive oil
30ml (2tbsp) breadcrumbs

Cook the pasta in the usual way, then drain in a colander and run it under cold water to stop cooking. Drain it really well, shaking the colander hard to remove every last drop of water. Now turn it out onto a large, flat dish which will hold the pasta in something like a single layer, and toss gently with a little bit of oil. This will help keep the pasta from sticking together if it's to be left for a while. Do not refrigerate but try to use within an hour or so of cooking.

Meanwhile, de-seed and coarsely chop the tomatoes, cucumber and peppers. Finely chop the onion and garlic, and quarter the olives. Put the spices in a pestle and grind till medium-fine, or just crush them with the back of a spoon. Add to the vegetables and pour in half the oil, using just enough to make a very thick sludge. Season with salt and pepper, and refrigerate for at least four hours.

When you're ready to serve, heat the remaining oil in a frying pan and fry the breadcrumbs till they're golden and crisp. Meanwhile, spread the gazpacho mixture over the pasta. When the crumbs are done, scatter them over the dish and serve immediately.

Pasta Salad with Marinated Salmon

You can also use smoked haddock or cod. Get the fishmonger to slice the fillets for you

500g (1lb 2oz) short pasta, such as fusilli or penne
450g (1lb) smoked salmon, haddock or cod, skinned and
sliced around 5mm (¼in) thick
45ml (3tbsp) extra virgin olive oil
15ml (1tbsp) balsamic vinegar
juice of ½ a lemon
1 spring onion, finely chopped
small handful fresh herbs – chervil, parsley,
dill or a combination

Cook the pasta in the usual way, then drain in a colander and run it under cold water to stop cooking. Drain it really well, shaking the colander hard to remove every last drop of water. Now turn it out onto a large, flat dish which will hold the pasta in something like a single layer, and toss gently with a little bit of oil. This will help keep the pasta from sticking together if it's to be left for a while. Do not refrigerate but try to use within an hour or so of cooking.

Lay the slices of fish on a large serving platter or tray in as even a layer as you can manage. Make a marinade from the oil, vinegar, lemon, spring onions, and season with salt and pepper. Brush and spoon over the fish and refrigerate for anything between 30 minutes and a couple of hours. Tear leaves into small pieces and toss with the walnut or hazelnut oil plus a pinch of salt. Refrigerate till needed, remembering to remove the fish around 20 minutes before you want to eat. Just before serving, chop the herbs and mix with the pasta, then lay on the fish. Drizzle on a little more olive oil (if you wish), and serve immediately.

Pink Pasta Salad

If you can't find radicchio, or if it's too expensive, red oak leaf lettuce would make a pretty good substitute to preserve the colour. Failing that, watercress is your best bet.

500g (1lb 2oz) short pasta, such as penne or fusilli
2-4 red peppers
2-4 red, ripe tomatoes
2 heads radicchio
60ml (4tbsp) extra virgin olive oil
10ml (2tsp) balsamic vinegar
10ml (2tsp) red wine vinegar

At least two hours before you want to eat, grill the peppers until they're soft and somewhat blackened all over (around 10-15 minutes). Leave to cool a little, then pull off the skins, de-seed, and cut into strips. Cover and refrigerate. Boil a pan of water and dip in the tomatoes for ten seconds, then peel, halve, de-seed, and cut into strips. Cover and refrigerate.

Cook the pasta in the usual way, then drain in a colander and run it under cold water to stop cooking. Drain it really well, shaking the colander hard to remove every last drop of water. Now turn it out onto a large, flat dish which will hold the pasta in something like a single layer, and toss gently with a little bit of oil. This will help keep the pasta from sticking together if it's to be left for a while. Do not refrigerate but try to use within an hour or so of cooking.

Trim the radicchio, separate the leaves, and rinse and dry well. Put in a plastic bag and refrigerate. Make a vinaigrette from the remaining ingredients plus some salt and pepper. Just before serving, tear the leaves into bite-sized pieces. Mix all the veg with the pasta, drizzle on the dressing, and serve immediately.

Pasta Salad with Herbed Crème Fraîche

This would also be good on cold fish or chicken. It can be turned into a low-cal dip by using yoghurt instead of crème fraîche.

500g (1lb 2oz) short pasta, such as penne or fusilli
45ml (3tbsp) extra virgin olive oil
200ml (7fl oz) crème fraîche
15ml (1tbsp) red wine vinegar
15ml (1tbsp) balsamic vinegar
2 shallots or spring onions
small handful fresh herbs, e.g. basil, coriander and parsley

Cook the pasta in the usual way, then drain in a colander and run it under cold water to stop cooking. Drain it really well, shaking the colander hard to remove every last drop of water. Now turn it out onto a large, flat dish which will hold the pasta in something like a single layer, and toss gently with a little bit of oil. This will help keep the pasta from sticking together if it's to be left for a while. Do not refrigerate but try to use within an hour or so of cooking.

Finely chop the shallots/spring onions and the herbs. Combine all ingredients except the herbs in a mixing bowl. (May be prepared up to an hour in advance up to this point.) Just before serving, coarsely chop the herbs and stir them in well. Toss with the cooked pasta, and serve immediately.

Pasta Salad with Ginger, Carrots and Tomotoes

This is a refreshing summer meal, but a substantial one as well. The quantities given below would serve at least six people as a side dish.

500g (1lb 2oz) short pasta, such as penne or fusilli
450g (1lb) young carrots
2 spring onions or 1 small red onion
1 large knob peeled ginger
60ml (4tbsp) extra virgin olive oil
juice of 1 lime or ½ a lemon
2 ripe tomatoes
10ml (2tsp) balsamic vinegar

Cook the pasta in the usual way, then drain in a colander and run it under cold water to stop cooking. Drain it really well, shaking the colander hard to remove every last drop of water. Now turn it out onto a large, flat dish which will hold the pasta in something like a single layer, and toss gently with a little bit of oil. This will help keep the pasta from sticking together if it's to be left for a while. Do not refrigerate but try to use within an hour or so of cooking.

Meanwhile, peel and grate the carrots or chop into very fine julienne strips. (This takes ages – grating is easier.) Thinly slice the onion/spring onion, and chop the ginger either in thin shreds or tiny chunks. Combine with the carrots in a glass or plastic bowl, season well with salt and pepper, and dress with half the oil and the lime/lemon juice. Add a little more oil if the carrots seem dry.

When you're ready to serve, core the tomatoes and slice thinly; you can de-seed them if you wish and cut into shreds instead, which would look somewhat neater. Toss with the balsamic vinegar and a little salt and pepper. Now toss the carrots with the pasta, top with the tomato slices, drizzle on the remaining extra virgin olive oil, and serve.

Pasta Salad with Tomato, Mozzarella and Basil

This takes one of the most popular dinner-party starters and turns it into a substantial main course. It can be prepared well in advance but the final stage – tearing the basil and assembling the ingredients – should not be done till just before serving. The best mozzarella to use is the Italian type, sold in plastic bags weighing around 125-150g (5-6oz). Serves four-six people.

500g (1lb 2oz) short pasta, such as fusilli or penne
60-75ml (4-5 tbsp) extra virgin olive oil
3-4 packets of Italian mozzarella
4-5 large, red, ripe tomatoes
large handful fresh basil

Cook the pasta in the usual way, then drain in a colander and run it under cold water to stop cooking. Drain it really well, shaking the colander hard to remove every last drop of water. Now turn it out onto a large, flat dish which will hold the pasta in something like a single layer, and toss gently with a little bit of oil. This will help keep the pasta from sticking together if it's to be left for a while. Do not refrigerate but try to use within an hour or so of cooking.

Drain the cheeses well, then chop them into smallish dice around 1.5cm (½in) square. Cover and refrigerate till needed. Core the tomatoes and slice around 5mm (¼in) thick; cover and refrigerate.

Just before serving, chop or tear all but four or five leaves of the basil into small pieces. Toss with the pasta, cheese and remaining oil, and season well with black pepper and a little salt. Spread the pasta out on the serving platter, top with the tomatoes in neat rows, and garnish with the whole basil leaves. Serve immediately with a green salad.

Ratatouille Pasta Salad

This is a very simple dish, but it does take a lot of time to cook. You could easily simplify it for everyday purposes by omitting some of the vegetables (as long as you use onion and garlic). You could also easily serve it hot if you wish, by just reheating the veg and adding to the pasta straight out of the pot. If you make it as a salad, however, cook the veg first and the pasta last, as the veg will benefit from resting time and the pasta needs relatively little.

500g (1lb 2oz) short pasta such as penne or fusilli
1 large onion
4 cloves garlic
4 red and/or yellow peppers
500g (1lb) courgettes
1-2 medium aubergines
450g (1lb) red, ripe tomatoes
100ml (4fl oz) extra virgin olive oil
parsley for garnish (optional)

Do the veg preparation first of all (and there's a lot of it). Slice the onions, mince the garlic, halve and de-seed the peppers. Wash, top and tail the courgettes and aubergines. Core, halve, and de-seed the tomatoes. Cut everything into bite-sized pieces except the aubergines, which should be cut just before cooking.

Gently heat 15ml (1tbsp) of oil in a large frying pan, preferably nonstick, and stir-fry the onions and garlic for one minute. Add the peppers, turn the heat up a little, and cook till they're done but still quite crunchy (around five-ten minutes). If you like them softer, add another ten minutes to the cooking time. Remove to a bowl. Now put in a little more oil and cook the courgettes for around the same time, depending on how you like them done. I like a bit of charring here and there, so I tend to use a higher heat for three-five minutes. Some courgettes will be soft, some crunchy, and some will have brown spots. Add to the peppers.

Finally cook the aubergines. This is done in the same way, but they need more oil and they need to be cooked till they're truly soft. Allow 20 to 25 minutes, over a moderate heat, with frequent stirring and turning.

When the aubergines are ready, add the tomatoes to the pan and cook, without oil, just long enough to let them break down and become a little watery.

Put everything together and toss with olive oil to taste, plus a little lemon juice if you like.

Cook the pasta in the usual way, then drain in a colander and run it under cold water to stop cooking. Drain it really well, shaking the colander hard to remove every last drop of water. Now turn it out onto a large, flat dish which will hold the pasta in something like a single layer, and toss gently with a little bit of oil. This will help keep the pasta from sticking together if it's to be left for a while. Do not refrigerate but try to use within an hour or so of cooking.

When you're ready to serve, just mix the pasta with the ratatouille and taste for salt and pepper. Season further as needed, garnish with chopped parsley if you wish, and serve.

Asian Noodles

Basic Chinese-Style Noodles
Chinese Noodles with Spicy Minced Chicken
Stir-Fried Beef Noodles
Chilli Noodles with Butter-Fried Salmon
Chinese-Style Chicken Noodle Soup
Thai-Flavoured Noodles
Sesame Noodles
Noodles with Thai-Style Prawns
Egg Noodles with a Vegetarian Stir-Fry
Spaghetti with Thai-Flavoured Tomato Sauce
Noodles with Tomato-Braised Pork
Noodles with Hot and Sour Grilled Pork

The pasta cookery of Asia is every bit as good and as varied as that of Italy. It is also very complex at times, calling for large numbers of ingredients and a lot of preparation. I've concentrated on very informal, easy-going adaptations here, because the real thing is just too time-consuming for most home cooks. If you want to explore further, get a good specialist book. You'll need one for China, one for Thailand, one for Malaysia, and one for Japan (which I've largely ignored). That's a lot of book-buying, but there's a lot of noodle lore that needs absorbing! And it is worth the effort, without question . . .

Basic Chinese-Style Noodles

2-3 cloves garlic
1 large piece fresh ginger
2-3 spring onions
15ml (1tbsp) vegetable oil
30ml (2tbsp) sesame oil
15ml (1tbsp) soy sauce
1 x 250g (9oz) packet dried egg noodles

Peel the garlic and ginger, and chop finely along with the spring onions. Heat the vegetable oil and stir-fry the chopped ingredients over a medium heat till they're softened slightly and very fragrant (around two-three minutes). May be prepared in advance to this point.

Cook the noodles in plenty of salted water till they're just done – they should not be overcooked. Meanwhile, reheat the garlic etc. over a low heat if they have been cooked in advance. When the noodles are done, drain well and add to the pan. Add the sesame oil and soy sauce, toss thoroughly, and serve immediately. This will serve two people as a main course, four as a side dish.

Chinese Noodles with Spicy Minced Chicken

This takes the basic recipe and turns it into a delicious main course.

2 boneless chicken breasts or 4-6 boneless thighs
15-30ml (1-2tbsp) vegetable oil
1 fresh chilli, or 5-10ml (1-2tsp) chilli sauce
15ml (1tbsp) Worcester sauce
15ml (1tbsp) tomato ketchup
2-3 cloves garlic
1 large piece fresh ginger
2-3 spring onions
15ml (1tbsp) vegetable oil
30ml (2tbsp) sesame oil
15ml (1tbsp) soy sauce
1 x 250g (9oz) packet dried egg noodles

Season the chicken with salt and pepper. Heat enough vegetable oil in a large frying pan to film the bottom, and get the pan very hot. Put in the chicken pieces and cook, turning once, till they're deeply browned on both sides and just cooked through (around 10-15 minutes for breasts, 5-10 for thighs). Remove to a plate while you de-seed and finely chop the chilli (if using) and measure out the Worcester sauce and ketchup. When the chicken is cool, chop it to the consistency of ordinary mince. Mix with the chilli, Worcester sauce and ketchup, and leave to marinate, covered, till you're ready to eat.

Peel the garlic and ginger, and chop finely along with the spring onions. Heat the vegetable oil and stir-fry the chopped ingredients over a medium heat till they're softened slightly and very fragrant (around two-three minutes). May be prepared in advance to this point.

Cook the noodles in plenty of salted water till they're just done – they should not be overcooked. Meanwhile, reheat the garlic etc. over a low heat if they have been cooked in advance. When the noodles are done, drain well and add to the pan. Add the sesame oil and soy sauce, toss thoroughly, and top with the minced chicken. Serve immediately. This will serve four people as a main course.

Stir-Fried Beef Noodles

Marinating the beef will improve the flavour, but it's not strictly necessary if you're pressed for time.

250g (9oz) packet dried Chinese egg noodles
350g (12oz) shredded beef
30ml (2tbsp) dry sherry or white wine
3 cloves garlic
1 big piece of fresh ginger
1 red or green chilli
2-3 spring onions or shallots
2-3 stalks celery
2-3 carrots
15ml (1tbsp) vegetable oil
15ml (1tbsp) sesame oil
15ml (1tbsp) soy sauce

If you have time to marinate the beef, put it in a bowl with the sherry or wine. Finely chop the garlic, ginger (peeled), and spring onions/shallots, and mix with the beef. Marinate for as long as you can — at least 15 minutes if possible. Meanwhile, thinly slice the celery and carrots.

Boil a large pot of water for the pasta. Heat the vegetable oil in a large frying pan or a wok, and stir-fry the celery and carrots over a brisk heat for one-two minutes. Now get the pasta cooking, and add the beef mixture to the pan. If you haven't marinated, just add the beef with the flavourings. Stir-fry briskly until the beef is cooked and turn off the heat. Drain the pasta well, add to the pan with the sesame oil and soy sauce, and toss well. Serve immediately.

Chilli Noodles with Butter-Fried Salmon

You could cook the salmon in oil, but butter is better.

1 clove garlic
1 large piece fresh ginger
2-3 spring onions
1 small green or red chilli
15ml (1tbsp) vegetable oil
15ml (1tbsp) sesame oil
5ml (1tsp) oyster sauce
15ml (1tbsp) soy sauce
1 x 250g (9oz) packet dried egg noodles
2 salmon fillets, skinless
1 large knob butter
small handful coriander

Peel the garlic and ginger, and chop finely along with the spring onions. De-seed the chilli and chop it too very finely. Mix with the oils, soy sauce and oyster sauce.

Boil a large pot of water for the noodles, and cook till they're just done – they should not be overcooked. Meanwhile, melt the butter in a nonstick pan and cook the salmon gently, on one side only, till the under-side is crusty and brown and the top retains a good hint of pink (around six-eight minutes). If you don't like rare salmon, you can turn the fillets at the end of cooking for one minute, which should be plenty of time to cook them through. While the fish is cooking, chop the coriander very finely.

Toss the cooked noodles with the dressing, then divide it between the two plates. Put a salmon fillet on each one, sprinkle with coriander, and serve immediately.

Chinese-Style Chicken Noodle Soup

Make sure the stock is hot when you add the stir-fried ingredients to it.

2-3 cloves garlic
1 large piece fresh ginger
2-3 spring onions
450ml (¾ pint) chicken stock
225g (8oz) chicken shreds
15ml (1tbsp) vegetable oil
30ml (2tbsp) sesame oil
15ml (1tbsp) soy sauce
1 x 250g (9oz) packet dried egg noodles

Peel the garlic and ginger, and chop finely along with the spring onions. Bring the stock to a steady simmer in a saucepan. Heat the vegetable oil and stir-fry the chopped ingredients with the chicken over a medium heat till the chicken is barely cooked through (around two-three minutes). Add to the chicken stock and keep at a low simmer for a couple of minutes.

Meanwhile, cook the noodles in plenty of salted water till they're just done – they should not be overcooked. When the noodles are ready, drain well and divide between two large bowls. Divide the chicken and its stock between the bowls, add the sesame oil and soy sauce, and serve immediately. This will serve two people as a main course, and can be garnished with chopped coriander, spring onions, or chilli sauce.

Thai-Flavoured Noodles

This also goes well with chicken and pork.

450g (1lb) egg noodles
3 thick slices ginger
4 kaffir lime leaves
1 stalk lemon grass
1 plump clove garlic
1 red pepper
large handful fresh coriander
30ml (2tbsps) vegetable oil
30ml (2tbsps) sesame oil
5ml (1tsp) red wine vinegar
2.5ml (½tsp) Thai fish sauce
5ml (1tsp) soy sauce

Boil a large pot of water for the noodles and get them cooking. Meanwhile, prepare the ingredients as follows: peel and mince the ginger, finely shred the lime leaves, mince the lemon grass and garlic, de-seed the pepper and cut into thin shreds, coarsely chop the coriander. Heat the vegetable oil in a medium frying pan and stir-fry all prepared ingredients except the coriander for one-two minutes. Toss with the cooked, drained noodles plus the sesame oil, vinegar and fish sauce. Mix in the coriander and serve immediately. This can be a side dish or a vegetarian main course.

Sesame Noodles

This can be eaten hot or at room temperature, and the vegetables can be varied as you please. A meal in itself, or a great side dish for plainly cooked chicken.

3 spring onions or 1 small onion
2 green peppers
2 medium carrots
125g (4oz) bean sprouts (optional)
30ml (2tbsp) vegetable oil
350g (12oz) dried Chinese egg noodles
Dressing:
30ml (2tbsps) sesame paste
80ml (3fl oz) soy sauce
15ml (1tbsp) sesame oil
45ml (3tbsps) red wine vinegar
chilli sauce to taste (optional)
5ml (1tsp) sugar

Slice the onion thinly or, if using spring onions, into thin shreds. De-seed the peppers. Peel the carrots and slice very thinly on the bias.

Heat half the vegetable oil in a wok or large frying pan and stir-fry the vegetables (except bean sprouts) till slightly softened (around five minutes). Add the bean sprouts, toss well, and turn the heat off. Bring a large pot of water to a boil and cook the noodles. Meanwhile, whisk the dressing ingredients with the remaining vegetable oil. When the noodles are cooked, drain well and toss with the dressing.

If eating hot, top with the vegetables and serve immediately. If serving as a salad, spread out on a serving platter to cool and then refrigerate. But remember to take out of the fridge an hour or so before serving, as some of the flavour will be lost if the dish is served too cold.

Noodles with Thai-Style Prawns

Thai or Vietnamese fish sauce and lime leaves are sold by many supermarkets and every shop specialising in Asian foods. You could also use cold chicken for this dish. It is spicy and pungent, perfect for eating with icy lager.

250g (9oz) packet dried Chinese egg noodles
450g (1lb) cooked prawns, in the shell
1 small chilli
1 clove garlic
2 shallots or 1 small red onion
2 lime leaves
30ml (2tbsp) sesame oil
15ml (1tbsp) vegetable oil
45ml (3tbsp) chicken stock
30ml (2tbsp) Thai or Vietnamese fish sauce
30ml (2tbsp) lemon juice
1 spring onion, finely shredded
small handful fresh coriander

Defrost the prawns if necessary and remove the heads but leave the shells on (for a nicer colour). De-seed the chillies and finely chop with the garlic. Slice the shallots/red onion as thinly as possible. Remove the central stalk from the lime leaves and cut into thin shreds. Mix these ingredients with the oils, stock, fish sauce and lemon juice, and marinate the prawns in the mixture for at least 20 minutes.

Boil a large pot of water for the noodles and get them cooking. Meanwhile, finely chop the coriander and spring onion. When the noodles are cooked, toss well with the marinated prawns and garnish with the spring onion and coriander. May be served hot or at room temperature.

Egg Noodles with a Vegetarian Stir-Fry

375g (12oz) French beans
3 medium carrots
2 stalks celery
4 spring onions
6 thin slices of ginger, peeled
2-3 cloves garlic
10ml (2tsp) vegetable oil
15ml (1tbsp) soy sauce
60ml (4tbsp) chicken or vegetable stock
30ml (2tbsp) dry sherry, or dry white wine or vermouth
5ml (1tsp) sesame oil
250g (9oz) packet dried Chinese egg noodles

Boil a large pot of water for the noodles. Meanwhile, top and tail the beans. Peel the carrots and slice around 5mm (¼in) thick. Trim the celery and slice to the same thickness. Top and tail the spring onions, and cut on the bias into thick shreds. Chop the garlic and ginger very finely.

Get the vegetable oil very hot in a wok or large frying pan, and stir-fry the vegetables till they're well softened but still retain a hint of bite (around three-four minutes). Add the soy sauce, stock and wine, and cook down till almost evaporated. May be prepared in advance to this point and left in the pan for up to 30 minutes.

Cook the noodles according to the instructions on the packet, then drain well. Add to the vegetables, heat thoroughly but quickly, and mix in the sesame oil. Serve immediately, with an extra sprinkling of chopped spring onions or coriander if you wish.

Noodles with Tomato-Braised Pork

This will serve six people easily, or even eight-ten if you double the quantity of noodles.

250g (9oz) packet dried Chinese egg noodles
4 strips of lean belly of pork (about 675g, 1lb 8oz)
30ml (2tbsp) peanut oil
2 cloves garlic
3 slices ginger
1 small chilli
450g (1lb) white or green cabbage
15ml (1tbsp) Worcester sauce
15ml (1tbsp) tomato ketchup
15ml (1tbsp) red wine vinegar
15ml (1tbsp) soy sauce
225ml (8 fl oz) chicken stock
1 x 400g (14oz) tin chopped tomatoes
5ml (1tsp) tomato paste
spring onions or fresh coriander to garnish

Preheat the oven to 170°C (325°F, Gas Mark 3) and bring two litres of water to boil in a casserole. Meanwhile, cut the pork into large chunks and finely chop the garlic, bay leaf, and chilli. When the water's boiled in the casserole, put in the pork and simmer for three minutes, then drain in a colander. Return the casserole to the heat and add the oil. Gently fry the garlic, bay leaf, and chilli for a minute or so. Slice the cabbage into bite-sized pieces and add to the casserole with pork and all remaining ingredients. Season with salt and pepper, stir well, and bring to the boil. Cover and cook in the oven for two hours or so, stirring occasionally. Skim well to remove excess fat. May be prepared in advance to this point, even a day before you're serving it.

Boil a large pot of water for the noodles, reheat the pork over a moderate heat, and get the noodles cooking. Meanwhile, finely chop the spring onions or coriander. When the noodles are done, drain well and mix in a big bowl or serving platter with a ladleful of sauce from the pork. Top with the remaining ingredients of the casserole, sprinkle with the spring onions or coriander, and serve immediately.

Spaghetti with Thai-Flavoured Tomato Sauce

This sauce is also delicious on hamburgers.

500g (1lb 2oz) spaghetti
1 small green chilli
3 kaffir lime leaves
2 cloves garlic
4-5 thin slices fresh ginger
1 stalk lemon grass
30ml (2tbsp) vegetable oil
1 x 400g (14oz) tin chopped plum tomatoes
juice of ½ a lemon
6-8 leaves sweet basil or Thai hot basil

De-seed the chilli, then chop it very finely with all remaining ingredients except the tomatoes and basil. Heat the oil in a frying pan and fry gently for a minute or so. Add the tomatoes and lemon juice, bring to a boil, then turn down the heat and simmer gently for 25-30 minutes.

Boil a large pot of water for the pasta and get it cooking. Meanwhile, chop the basil. When the pasta is done, drain well and toss with the sauce and the basil. Serve immediately.

Noodles with Hot and Sour Grilled Pork

This is a party dish of sorts, in the sense that it takes a little advance planning and serves four people. But you could also make it on a week night, and use chicken, lamb, duck, or beef instead of pork.

500g (1lb 2oz) pork, in thick chunks
2 cloves garlic
5ml (1tsp) chilli sauce
30ml (2tbsp) red wine vinegar or lemon juice
15ml (1tbsp) soy sauce
10ml (2tsp) sugar
250g (9oz) packet dried egg noodles
1 green and 1 red pepper
3-4 spring onions
30ml (2tbsp) sesame oil

Put the pork in a large glass or ceramic bowl. Finely chop the garlic, then mix with the next four ingredients till the sugar is dissolved. Pour this over the pork, season with black pepper, toss well, and leave to marinate for 30 minutes at least (and overnight if you are able).

When you're getting ready to cook, drain the pork well of marinade and thread onto four skewers. Boil a large pot of water for the noodles. Cook the pork under a hot grill, turning three-four times, till it's done but not dried out (around 10-15 minutes). Heat the marinade to boiling point in a small saucepan, and set aside.

Get the noodles cooking, and de-seed the peppers and cut into thin shreds. Cut the sopping onions into thin discs or shreds. When the noodles are done, toss with the cooked marinade and sesame oil. Divide between four plates or bowls and put a skewer on each one. Sprinkle over the spring onions, and perhaps an extra dash of soy sauce, and serve immediately.

Party Dishes

Dead-Easy Tomato Sauce
Dead-Easy Meat Sauce
Honey Roasted Chicken with Spicy Noodles
Easy-Cooking Leg of Lamb with Garlic and Macaroni
Braised Duck Legs with Orzo
Spaghetti with American-Style Chilli
Spaghetti with Mussels
Spaghetti with a Roasted Vegetable Platter
Winter Soup
Spaghetti with Meatballs and Sausages
Caramelised Onion Sauce
Creamy Chicken Linguini
Spicy Pork Chop
Pot-Roasted Beef on a bed of Spaghetti
Spaghetti with 40 Cloves of Garlic
Paella-Style Pasta
Prawn Sauce with Lemon Grass
Basic Macaroni Cheese
Baked Pasta and Sweetcorn
Fancy Macaroni Cheese
Gratin 'Parmigiana'
Cheat's Lasagne
1-2-3 Baked Macaroni

Everyone throws a dinner party every once in a while. Or at least I hope they (read: you) do. A dinner party doesn't have to be a formal, nervous, grown-up affair where everyone's on best behaviour. It can be as raucous and irreverent as a night spent clubbing. The difference is that there's food involved, and if there's food, you want it to be a cut above what you eat every other night of the week. That's where these recipes come in. They take a bit more time, or a lot more time in some cases. They may also cost more because – well, because your friends deserve the best.

Having said all that, I should add immediately that the cooking here has been kept to a minimum, both in quantity and in difficulty. Some dishes are just time-consuming, and you can't get round it. But others are almost as simple as those in the first chapter. While they may take more time, much of that time will be spent cooking something else, or washing up, or even – God forbid – enjoying yourself.

Dead-Easy Tomato Sauce

These quantities make more sauce than you will need immediately, unless you're serving a big crowd. The leftovers will keep well in the fridge for a week or more, and in the freezer indefinitely.
The basic recipe is simplicity itself, and the variations take hardly any more time. This quantity will sauce two pounds of pasta, so you'll probably have some for the freezer.

2 x 400g (14oz) tins Italian plum tomatoes
1 small onion
2 cloves garlic
1 small carrot
½ stick of celery
30ml (2tbsp) extra-virgin olive oil
30ml (2tbsp) tomato paste or purée
fresh or dried herbs of your choice
grated Parmesan for serving

Roughly chop the tomatoes in their tins with a table knife. Peel the onion and garlic, and wash the carrot and celery well. Mince them together or chop in a food processor. Heat the oil in a saucepan and gently cook the vegetables for five minutes, then add the tomatoes, the paste or puree, and the herbs. Season well with salt and pepper, bring to a boil, then turn down the heat and simmer gently for anything from 30 to 90 minutes. The cooking time will depend on how much time you have and how thick a sauce you want. Serve with four-five tbsp of freshly grated Parmesan.

Variations

For extra richness, add a thick pat of butter to the oil and swirl in 50ml (around 3tbsp) of double cream before serving.

Just before serving, toast 25-50g (1-2oz) of pine nuts in a dry frying pan till they're lightly golden-brown. Sprinkle onto the sauced pasta in its serving bowl.

If you eat meat, add 50-75g (2-3oz) of bacon or ham during the first cooking of the onions etc.

Add four minced anchovy fillets, 1 sun-dried tomato, 1tsp of balsamic vinegar, and a little chilli powder when you start cooking the vegetables.

Stirring in a small handful of chopped capers or good olives adds a nice sharpness. If you can find fresh fennel, chop a small bulb and add it to the minced onions etc. before cooking.

Dead-Easy Meat Sauce

This is based very roughly on the classic Bolognese meat sauce called ragu, but it takes far less work. Ask the butcher to cut up the beef for you if you don't feel like doing it at home – but don't worry if you have to do it yourself, because it only takes a few minutes.

450g (1lb) braising steak or shoulder of pork
10ml (2tsp) vegetable oil
2 large Spanish onions
2-3 cloves garlic
1 small dried red chilli (optional)
5ml (1tsp) dried mixed herbs, or a single herb such as rosemary or oregano
pinch each of cinnamon and nutmeg (optional)
100ml (6-7tbsp) dry wine, red or white
2 x 400g (14oz) tins plum tomatoes

If you're cutting up the meat yourself, use a large, sharp knife on a large cutting board. Trim away any loose fat and connective tissue, and slice the meat across the grain into very thin slices (around 2.5mm or ⅛in thick), then cut each slice into shreds. Don't worry about making them exactly the same size or thickness: they'll cook down just the same. When half are done, put them in a big, heavy pot with the oil and start cooking over a medium heat to colour them a little while you prepare the rest. Add them to the pot and keep cooking, stirring every few minutes.

Meanwhile, prepare the onions and garlic by peeling and slicing them very thin; the onions should be halved before slicing. Add to the pot with the chilli (if using), give everything a good stir, and cook for a few minutes more. Now add the wine and tomatoes, bring to a boil, then turn down the heat and cover the pot. Simmer it very gently for two hours or so; if the pot can go into the oven, that's a good place to cook the sauce. Use a heat of 150°C (300°F, Gas Mark 2) for one-two hours, stirring every fifteen minutes or so.

Honey Roasted Chicken with Spicy Noodles

This is an unusual dish in combining pasta with Middle Eastern flavours. Serves four people.

4 chicken pieces, breast or leg
15ml (1tbsp) runny honey
1 medium onion
1 clove of garlic
1 small chunk of fresh ginger
1 small dried or fresh chilli, seeds removed
large knob butter
5ml (1tsp) cumin seeds
5ml (1tsp) coriander seeds
60ml (4 tbsp) dry white wine or vermouth
500g (1lb 2oz) short pasta
60ml (4tbsp) extra virgin olive oil

Preheat the oven to 200°C (400°F, Gas Mark 6). Brush the chicken pieces with the honey, season with salt and pepper, then put them on a rack in a roasting tin with a splash of water. Roast on a middle shelf for around 30 minutes (for breasts) or 40 minutes (for legs). Baste a few times during cooking.

Meanwhile, finely chop the onions, garlic, ginger and chilli. Melt the butter in a small saucepan over a low heat, and cook the onions etc. to soften them without colouring (around five minutes). Now add the spices and continue cooking for a minute or two, then pour in the wine and cook gently till it's completely evaporated. Turn off the heat and leave till you're ready to serve.

Boil a large pot of water for the pasta and get it cooking. Gently reheat the spice mixture, adding the olive oil just long enough to heat it through. Toss the sauce with the cooked, drained pasta, and serve on heated plates with one chicken piece per person.

Easy-Cooking Leg of Lamb with Garlic and Macaroni

This dish is based on the French dish called 'Gigot à quatre heures' or 'à sept heures'. The idea is to cook the meat till it's tender enough to cut with a spoon, then reduce the sauce and toss the cooked pasta in it before serving. Incredibly easy and fantastically delicious. If you are not a garlic fanatic, reduce the amount by half or even a quarter.

500g (1lb 2oz) macaroni
2-3 kilo (4lb) leg of lamb
30ml (2tbsp) vegetable oil
2 heads of garlic
1 large onion
1 large carrot
2 stalks celery
1 x 400g (14oz) tin of tomatoes
3-4 peppercorns
1 bay leaf
a small handful of parsley
5ml (1tsp) dried mixed herbs
1 75cl metric bottle of white wine

Preheat the oven to 180°C (350°F, Gas 4). Heat the oil in a very large frying pan and brown the lamb as evenly as possible (around 10-15 minutes); transfer it to a large casserole. Meanwhile, separate the garlic cloves but leave them unpeeled. Coarsely chop the onion, carrots and celery, and add to the casserole with all remaining ingredients plus enough wine to cover the lamb around halfway.

Bring to the boil on top of the hob, then cover and cook in the oven, turning occasionally; add more wine if too much is cooking away. A large leg will need six-seven hours, though it can be eaten any time from four hours onwards.

When the lamb is done, remove it from the pot and put on a serving platter covered with aluminium foil. Skim off every bit of fat from the cooking liquid; this may be easier if you strain it into a smaller pot or a bowl. Boil a large pot of water for the pasta and get it cooking while you boil down the cooking liquid to make around 225ml (8fl oz) of concentrated gravy. When the pasta is cooked, drain well and toss thoroughly in the cooking liquid. Serve the meat with the pasta, garlic and a green salad.

Braised Duck Legs with Orzo

Orzo is a tiny rice-shaped pasta. If you can't find it, the smallest tubes or shells will do very well. Duck legs are often sold (more cheaply than the breasts) in supermarkets and good butchers. The duck can be cooked a day in advance, and will actually benefit from cooking, chilling in the fridge, and gentle reheating the next day. Serves four people.

4 duck legs
1 big Spanish onion
2 cloves garlic
225ml (8fl oz) dry white wine or vermouth
30ml (2tbsp) red wine vinegar
5ml (1tsp) dried mixed herbs
small handful fresh parsley
350g (12oz) orzo or another small pasta

Prick the skin on the duck legs with a fork to help release fat as they cook, and season with salt and pepper. Put them, skin side down, in a large nonstick frying pan. Turn the heat on medium-hot and fry until the skin is well browned (around ten minutes). Meanwhile, slice the onions and garlic thinly. As the duck legs cook, spoon off the melting fat (and save it for making the most delicious fried potatoes you could ever imagine). When they're brown on the skin side, turn and brown the meaty side for one-two minutes. Remove to a casserole which will hold them in one or two layers.

Spoon out all but around 30ml (2tbsp) of duck fat from the frying pan. Put in the onions and garlic, and cook over a moderate heat till the onions are lightly coloured. Meanwhile, preheat the oven to 180°C (350°F, Gas Mark 4) if you're planning to cook the duck in the oven. When the onions are coloured, add to the casserole with the duck and put in the remaining ingredients. The dish may now be cooked in the oven for around 1-1¼ hours, or on the hob (over a very gentle heat) for around the same time. May be prepared in advance to this point. If cooking more than four hours in advance, leave to cool and refrigerate, and remove all traces of fat from the surface before reheating.

Boil a large pot of water for the pasta and get it cooking. Reheat the duck (if necessary), and finely chop the parsley. When the pasta is cooked, drain well and add to the casserole for a minute so it can absorb the delicious gravy. Serve immediately with a green vegetable.

Spaghetti with American-Style Chilli

This is based on the award-winning chilli recipe by 'Tarantula Jack' of Seattle, Washington. It is much better with rump steak, thinly sliced at home, but good mince will do if you don't feel like the extra work and expense.

500 g (1lb 2oz) spaghetti
450g (1lb) rump steak, or best mince
1 medium Spanish onion, grated or coarsely chopped
1 large clove garlic
30ml (2tbsp) vegetable oil
225ml (8fl oz) chicken stock
45ml (3tbsp) dry white wine or vermouth
1 x 400g (14oz) tin passata or Italian plum tomatoes
45ml (3tbsp) mild chilli powder
15ml (1tbsp) ground cumin
large pinch cayenne
mature Cheddar or Cheshire cheese for serving

If you're using rump steak, trim off all fat and slice around 2.5mm (⅛in) thick. Now cut each slice into shreds, also around 2.5mm (⅛in) thick and around 2.5cm (1in) long. Chop the onion and garlic finely. Heat the oil in a large frying pan and cook the beef quickly just until it loses its raw colour. Put it in a casserole with the onions and garlic, add the stock and wine, and simmer (covered) for 1½ hours.

Add the tomato sauce, chilli powder and ground cumin. Give everything a good stir and simmer gently for another hour. Check the pot from time to time to make sure there's enough liquid in it. If it seems to be too dry, add a little more wine, stock or water. Finally add the cayenne and cook for another fifteen minutes. May be prepared in advance to this point.

Boil a large pot of water for the pasta and get it cooking. Grate the cheese. When the pasta is cooked and drained, toss with a little butter and let everyone help themselves. You could also use Feta cheese for serving, crumbled rather than grated.

Spaghetti with Spicy Chicken Meatballs

1 clove garlic
150g (6oz) onion
450g (1lb) minced chicken
5ml (1tsp) whole cumin
5ml (1tsp) whole fenugreek
5ml (1tsp) whole coriander seeds
generous pinch of nutmeg
flour for frying
30ml (2 tbsp) vegetable oil
1 x 400g (14oz) tin tomatoes
15ml (1tbsp) tomato puree
100ml (4 floz) white wine or chicken stock
500g (1lb 2oz) spaghetti (or linguine or tagliatelle)
small handful fresh parsley or coriander

Chop the garlic and onion finely, mix with the chicken and spices, and season with salt and pepper. Form into four meatballs of equal size, and roll them in flour to cover uniformly. Heat the onion a large frying pan and fry till well browned (around five minutes). Now put the meatballs in a casserole just large enough to hold them in a single layer. Put in the tomatoes and tomato puree. Bring to the boil, turn down heat to medium-low, and simmer for around 40 minutes.

Boil a large pot of water for the pasta and get it cooking. Chop the parsley/coriander finely. When the pasta's cooked and drained, toss with a little butter, then dish out on heated plates with the sauce (one meatball per person) on top.

Spaghetti with Mussels

500g (1lb 2oz) spaghetti
2 kilo (4lb) bag of mussels
2 large cloves garlic
1 medium onion or 3-4 spring onions
5ml (1tsp) dried thyme
45ml (3 tbsp) extra virgin olive oil or 2 large knobs butter
200ml (around 7fl oz) dry white wine or sherry
100ml (around 3½fl oz) double cream (optional)
small handful parsley

Clean the mussels, discarding any that are open (and remain that way if you rap it hard on the sink). Mince the onions and garlic and put in a bowl. Mince the parsley and put in a separate bowl.

Boil a large pot of water for the pasta and get it cooking. Heat the butter/oil in a big pot or a wok and stir-fry the onions and garlic for a minute over a low heat. Add the mussels and thyme, and season well with salt and pepper. Toss well, then add the wine and stir again. Cover the pan and cook for six-eight minutes, tossing every minute or so. Meanwhile, chop the parsley coarsely. Stir in the cream if using and the parsley, and turn off the heat if the pasta isn't done yet. When it is done, drain well and toss with a little butter, then serve in big bowls and let your guests help themselves to mussels. The mussels should sit on top, and everyone should eat with their fingers. Provide plenty of napkins.

Spaghetti with a Roasted Vegetable Platter

This dish takes time but no effort – and no more skill than frying an egg. It's just a sumptuous platter of roasted vegetables served on a bed of spaghetti, so your guests can help themselves. The vegetables can be cooked well in advance and reheated in the oven if you like. I've given it here in quantities serving eight-ten people, since it's such a good party dish, but you could easily make it for four or even two.

500g (1lb 2oz) spaghetti
450g (1lb) red, ripe tomatoes
450g (1lb) courgettes
450g (1lb) aubergines, not too big
45ml (3tbsp) extra virgin olive oil, plus extra for cooking
15ml (1tbsp) balsamic vinegar
fresh herbs for garnish, e.g. basil, rosemary or mint

Preheat the oven to 200°C (400°F, Gas Mark 6). Put enough oil in a roasting tin to make a thin film, then halve the tomatoes and put them in the pan with the cut sides up. Drizzle on a little more oil and roast until lightly browned and very soft (around 30 minutes). Remove to a platter, taking care not to let them fall apart (they'll be pretty soft). Now repeat the process with the courgettes, which need around 15 minutes, and finally the aubergines, which should take 30 minutes or so. Cover the platter loosely with aluminium foil.

When you're ready, boil a large pot of water for the pasta and get it cooking. Reheat the veg if necessary in a low oven, whisk the 45ml (3tbsp) of oil with the vinegar and salt and pepper, and chop the herbs. When the pasta is cooked and drained, toss with a little more olive oil and put on a separate platter. Put the veg on top, drizzle on the vinaigrette and sprinkle on the herbs, and serve immediately with nothing more than a green salad (optional).

Winter Soup

Vary the vegetables you like, and use water at a pinch – but chicken stock, even from a cube, is really much, much better.

2 large cloves garlic
1 medium onion
100g (4oz) leeks, white part only
5ml (1tsp) dried herbs, e.g. thyme, rosemary or oregano,
or a mixture of all three
250g (8oz) carrots, chopped
Half a small cabbage
60ml (4tbsp) extra virgin olive oil
500ml (18fl oz) chicken stock
225g (8oz) small pasta, such as elbows
grated Parmesan for serving

Chop the garlic coarsely and slice the onion, leeks and carrot around 5mm (¼in) thick. Cut out the core from the cabbage and slice it around 2.5mm (⅛in) thick. Heat half the oil in a large casserole or saucepan, and cook the garlic, onion and leeks gently for a few minutes, then add the herbs, carrot and cabbage and season with salt and pepper. Continue cooking, stirring occasionally, for ten minutes or so, then add all remaining ingredients except the pasta. Bring to a boil and simmer gently until the vegetables are soft: this can take as little as 25-30 minutes if you want a bit of bite, or up to two hours if you want everything really mushy and well blended. When you're getting ready to eat, put in the pasta and cook at a good boil till the pasta is done. Serve with plenty of grated Parmesan.

Spaghetti with Meatballs and Sausages

An incredibly hearty dish. If you can't get Italian cooking sausages from a delicatessen, use smoked Polish- or Dutch-style sausages, or just well-flavoured bangers. Since this is a party dish, I've made it in quantities to serve eight.

460g (1lb) mince
1 small onion, finely chopped
5ml (1tsp) dried mixed herbs
60ml (4tbsp) extra virgin olive oil
450g (1lb) good sausages, cut into 2.5cm (1in) lengths
4 big cloves garlic, finely chopped
900g (2lb) tinned tomatoes
30ml (2 tbsp) tomato paste
100ml (4fl oz) dry white wine
10ml (2 tbsp) sugar
750g (1lb 8oz) spaghetti
grated Parmesan for serving

Combine the mince with the onion and herbs, and form into eight small meatballs. Get half the oil medium-hot in a large frying pan and brown the meatballs lightly. Remove to a plate and put in the sausages to brown in the same way.

Meanwhile, heat the remaining oil in a big saucepan and cook the garlic till it's fragrant and sizzling but not browned (around one minute). Add the tomatoes and tomato paste with plenty of salt and pepper, bring to the boil, and cook hard till the mixture is reduced by around one quarter.

When the sauce is reduced, add the meatballs, pasta, wine and sugar. Continue cooking at a gentle heat for at least 20 minutes and up to one hour, watching to make sure the sauce doesn't stick. If it does, add more wine.

Cook the pasta according to the instructions on the packet and drain into a large bowl. Pour on the sauce and take it to the table with bread, a salad and lots of wine. Grated Parmesan should be passed around separately.

Caramelised Onion Sauce

This is based on a recipe in Marcella Hazan's *Classic Italian Cooking*, and it is not just one of the best but one of the easiest pasta sauces around. The cooking can be done in the oven or on the hob.

500g (1lb 2oz) spaghetti
675g (1lb 8oz) onions
15ml (1tbsp) vegetable oil
60-75ml (4-5tbsp) extra virgin olive oil
grated Parmesan for serving

Peel the onions, halve lengthwise, and slice thinly.

To cook in the oven: preheat to 180°C (350°F, Gas Mark 4). Put the onions in a roasting tin, toss with the vegetable oil, and season with salt and pepper. Roast, stirring frequently, till the onions are well browned and completely soft (around 1½ hours).

To cook on the hob: put the onions in a large saucepan, toss with the vegetable oil, and season with salt and pepper. Cook over a low heat, stirring every few minutes, till the onions are well browned and completely soft (around one hour).

Cook the pasta till it's done *al dente* and toss with the onions plus the extra virgin olive oil. Serve with grated Parmesan.

Creamy Chicken Linguini

This is one of the few dishes in this book for which I have specified a particular pasta shape. Linguini just seem to work well with this luscious rich treatment.

500g (1lb 2oz) linguini
4 chicken legs or breasts, preferably free-range
a little flour
2-3 large knobs butter
225g (8oz) mushrooms
150ml (¼ pint) dry white wine or vermouth
150ml (¼ pint) chicken stock
300ml (½ pint) double cream
5ml (1tsp) dried tarragon
grated Parmesan for serving

Preheat the oven to 180°C (350°F, Gas Mark 4), and melt the butter in a large frying pan over a low heat. Season the chicken legs with salt and pepper, dust with flour, and brown lightly in butter (around 15 minutes). Arrange in a single layer in a roasting pan and cook in the oven till done (around 20 minutes). Meanwhile, clean the mushrooms and cut them in half if they are large. When the chicken is just cooked, drain off the excess butter and place the pan over a moderately high heat. Pour in the wine and cook for a minute or two, then turn the heat down and add the mushrooms, stock, cream and tarragon. Cook at a moderate heat for 15-20 minutes, constantly spooning the sauce over the chicken, until the sauce is thick. May be prepared up to 20 minutes in advance to this point. Meanwhile, cook the pasta *al dente* and drain well. When it's done, toss in the pan with the rich sauce and spoon onto four large plates. Put a piece of chicken on each plate, and serve immediately with grated Parmesan.

Spicy Pork Sauce

675g (1lb 8oz) cubed pork (e.g. shoulder or lean belly)
30ml (2tbsp) vegetable oil
2 cloves garlic
1 small chilli
1 large onion
1 bay leaf
15ml (1tbsp) Worcester sauce
15ml (1tbsp) red wine vinegar
225ml (8fl oz) chicken stock
1 x 400g (14oz) tin chopped plum tomatoes
15ml (1tbsp) tomato paste
a large pinch of thyme
500g (1lb 2oz) pasta

Preheat oven to 170°C (325°F, Gas Mark 3). Pat the pork dry on kitchen towels and heat the vegetable oil in a frying pan. Brown the meat in two batches till lightly coloured, then put in a casserole, draining off excess oil with a slotted spoon. Meanwhile, finely chop the garlic, chilli and onion. Add to the pot with all remaining ingredients. Season with salt and pepper, stir well, and bring to the boil. Cover and cook in the oven till the meat is soft (around two hours), stirring occasionally. May be prepared in advance to this point, even a day ahead of serving. When it is cool, skim well of surface fat. When you're getting ready to serve, boil a large pot of water for the pasta and get it cooking. Reheat the sauce gently in the meantime, making sure it gets hot but does not boil hard. Toss the cooked, drained pasta with the sauce, and serve (if you wish) with grated cheese.

Pot-Roasted Beef on a Bed of Spaghetti

The best thing about this dish – apart from deliciousness – is that it can be prepared completely the day before eating and reheated at the last moment. Indeed, it's better that way. If you don't eat beef, a shoulder of pork or lamb can be done in exactly the same way. This will serve 6-8 people, probably with plenty of delicious leftovers.

1.5kg (3lb) topside of beef, rolled
15-30ml (1-2tbsp) vegetable oil
2 large onions
4 stalks celery
4 medium carrots
4-5 cloves garlic
15ml (1tbsp) plain flour
10ml (2tsp) dried herbs, your choice
1 x 400g (14oz) tin of tomatoes
450ml (¾ pint) chicken or beef stock
around half a bottle of red wine
2-3 large knobs of butter
500g (1lb 2oz) spaghetti, or up to 750g (1lb 11oz) if you wish
small handful fresh parsley

Pat the meat dry while you heat the vegetable oil in a large frying pan which will hold the meat easily. Season the beef with salt and pepper and cook in the oil, turning as necessary, till it's browned all over (around 5-10 minutes). Meanwhile, you can prepare the vegetables: peel the onion and carrot, and slice everything into pieces around 1.5cm (½in) thick. Peel the garlic and slice thinly. Preheat the oven to 170C (325°F, Gas Mark 3).

When the meat is browned, turn the heat down to low and

transfer the meat to a large, heavy casserole. If there isn't enough oil and fat in the pan to coat the bottom easily, add another drizzle of oil. Now put the flour in and stir it well to break up clumps. When it is lightly coloured, add the vegetables and herbs, and cook just till the garlic becomes fragrant (around 2-3 minutes). Add to the casserole with the meat, then add the tomatoes, pour in all the stock and enough wine to cover the meat by around three quarters. Bring to the boil on the hob, cover, and put in the oven. Let it cook gently until it feels tender when pricked with a fork, around 2-3 hours. Turn it carefully once to ensure even cooking. Remove from the oven and leave to cool, uncovered, then put the lid back on and refrigerate overnight.

The next day, remove as much fat from the surface of the chilled beef as you can. Then take the meat out, scraping off all the sauce, and cut into thin slices. Taking care to keep the slices from falling to bits, return the meat to the casserole. This can be done well in advance of serving, as long as you refrigerate it again.

When you're around 1 hour from serving, preheat the oven to 140°C (275°F, Gas Mark 1). Put the casserole in and let the meat and sauce come back to a good heat. (If it's taking too long, turn the heat up a little bit.) Add the butter towards the end of reheating.

To serve: boil a large pot of water for the pasta and get it cooking. Chop the parsley if using. Remove the casserole from the oven when the pasta is nearly done, and have your serving utensils ready. When the pasta's cooked, drain it well and spread out on a huge serving platter. Carefully put the sliced meat on top, arranging as neatly as possible. Now spoon over every bit of sauce, top with the parsley if using, and take it to the table. Cheese is strictly optional with this dish, but serve if you have some around.

Spaghetti with 40 Cloves of Garlic

This is inspired by one of my all-time favourite dishes, Chicken with 40 Cloves of Garlic. it's definitely a party dish – and only when you're eating with friends who love garlic as much as you do.

80-100ml (3-4fl oz) extra virgin olive oil
4 or 5 heads of garlic
fresh herbs of your choice (e.g. sage, thyme, rosemary, tarragon)
grated Parmesan for serving
500g (1lb 2oz) spaghetti

Preheat oven to 180°C (350°F, Gas Mark 4). Separate the garlic into cloves, and remove the outer papery husks but do not peel them. Put the oil in a casserole or baking dish, then stir in the garlic, shaking the dish to make a single layer of cloves. Cover either with the lid or with aluminium foil, and bake till the garlic is completely soft (around 30-40 minutes). May be prepared in advance to this point.

Boil a large pot of water for the pasta and get it cooking. Chop the herbs. When the spaghetti is done, drain well and toss with the garlic and oil. You and your friends should eat the garlicky spaghetti while occasionally picking up a whole clove and sucking out the delicious, fragrant pulp. Can be served as a side dish, starter, or even a main course if you've had something substantial to start.

Paella-Style Pasta

675g (1½lb) short pasta such as fusilli or penne
10 chicken breasts, 20 drumsticks/thighs, or a combination
60-75ml (4-5tbsp) vegetable oil
1-2 Spanish onions, coarsely chopped
3-4 cloves garlic, finely chopped
2 stalks celery, thickly sliced
5ml (1tsp) paprika or ½ paprika and ½ cayenne
2 x 400g (14oz) tins plum tomatoes,
drained well and coarsely chopped
1 bay leaf
5ml (1tsp) dried thyme or tarragon
a splash of dry white wine or vermouth
long-grain rice to fill a 375ml (15fl oz) measuring cup
300ml (½pt) chicken stock

Advance preparation: If using chicken breasts, cut each one in half to make two roughly even-sized pieces. Dust the pieces with salt and black pepper, and heat half the oil in a large frying pan. If the pan is nonstick, you might be able to get away with using less oil. Brown the chicken pieces a few at a time, without crowding, transferring them to a large casserole as they're done.

Finely chop the onion, garlic and celery. Add the remaining oil to the pan and cook over a moderate heat till they're fragrant and slightly softened (around five minutes). Add the tomatoes, seasonings and wine, and cook hard for another few minutes to reduce the tomato to a thick sludge. Add to the casserole with the chicken, leave to cool, and then cover. May be prepared in advance to this point.

When you're ready to cook, preheat the oven to 180°C (350°F, Gas Mark 4). Pour in the stock, bring to the boil, cover, and cook in the oven for around one hour.

Meanwhile, boil a large pot of water for the pasta. When the chicken is around 10 minutes from being done, get it cooking. Drain well, then toss with the cooked chicken. Turn out onto a large platter and serve with green beans or a salad.

Prawn Sauce with Lemon Grass

This is actually a fairly quick dish to make, but I've put it in this chapter because the main ingredient is expensive and advance preparation is needed. You can buy uncooked prawns and cook them yourself, but the Tiger prawns widely (and expensively) sold in supermarkets are no better, in my view, than ordinary frozen Icelandic pre-cooked prawns. Be sure to start the preparation a few hours in advance.

500g (1lb 2oz) pasta
675g (1lb 8oz) frozen prawns
1 stalk lemon grass
2 cloves garlic
large knob butter
10ml (2tsp) tomato purée
225ml (8 floz) dry white wine or vermouth
45ml (3tbsp) double cream
2 spring onions for garnish

Defrost the prawns, then shell them. Put the prawns in the fridge, tightly covered, and set aside the shells. Coarsely chop the lemon grass and garlic, then put them in a saucepan with the butter and tomato puree. Cook over a gentle heat for a couple of minutes, till the garlic starts to sizzle a little, then add the wine/vermouth plus an equal amount of water. Bring to the boil, season with black pepper (no salt yet as the prawns may be salty), and simmer for 15 minutes. Now put the pan contents through a fine sieve into a clean saucepan. Simmer again till the liquid is reduced to around 100ml

(4fl oz). Leave to cool.

Boil a large pot of water for the pasta and get it cooking. Reheat the sauce gently, tasting for salt and adding some if needed, and finely chop the spring onions.

When the pasta is nearly done, add the prawns to the sauce with the cream, and heat through for just one minute. Toss the sauce with the cooked, drained pasta, sprinkle on the spring onions, and serve immediately.

Basic Macaroni Cheese

This is my version of the basic dish that everyone loves. It will serve 10-12.

30ml (2tbsp) softened butter
30ml (2tbsp) flour
60ml (l pint) milk
pinch of ground nutmeg
100g (4oz) Gruyère,
grated 300g (12oz) short pasta,such as fusilli or penne
45ml (3 tbsp) dry breadcrumbs
small handful parsley

First, make a béchamel sauce. Melt the butter over a low heat in a saucepan (nonstick is best) and stir in the flour with a wooden spoon. Cook, stirring constantly, for two-three minutes; the flour must not start to colour, but it must blend completely into the butter. Meanwhile, measure out the milk. Pour a little into the saucepan and stir constantly till it's absorbed. Add a little more and keep stirring till the extra milk's absorbed. Continue this process until the milk is all in; you can add it in larger doses towards the end. When all the milk is in, add the bay leaf and nutmeg, and turn the heat up a little so you get a steady, gentle simmer. The milk should not boil. Cook, stirring occasionally (and scraping the bottom of the pot for any stuck-on bits of flour) till the sauce is just thick enough to coat the back of your spoon. When it's reached this stage, leave to sit in the pan.

Meanwhile, boil a large pot of water for the pasta and get it cooking. Butter a large baking dish and preheat the oven to 200°C (400°F, Gas Mark 6).

When the pasta is cooked, drain well and put back in the pot.

Toss with the white sauce and all but a large spoonful of the cheese. Pour into the baking dish, sprinkle with the remaining cheese and the breadcrumbs, and bake near the top of the oven till the interior is bubbling and the top brown (around 25 minutes). Leave for a few minutes before serving.

Baked Pasta with Sweetcorn

This is a simple but delicious dish, perfect for a midweek dinner as well as a party.

2 x 200g (7oz) tins sweetcorn
500g (1lb 2oz) short pasta, such as fusilli or penne
3 eggs, beaten
200ml (⅓ pint) double cream
150ml (¼ pint) milk
150g (5oz) Cheddar or Cheshire cheese, grated

Preheat the oven to 200°C (400°F, Gas Mark 6), boil a large pot of water for the pasta, and drain the sweetcorn for a few minutes in a sieve. Meanwhile, beat the egg with the cream, milk and half the cheese, and butter a small baking dish. Cook the pasta till it's done *al dente*, then toss with the cream/milk/egg and the sweetcorn. Put in the baking dish, sprinkle on the remaining cheese, and dot with butter. Bake near the top of the oven till the top is brown (around 30 minutes). If the dish seems to be drying out before the top is brown, the browning can be completed under the grill.

Fancy Macaroni Cheese

This is perfect for a dinner party: it's luxurious but not too pricey.

30ml (2tbsp) softened butter
300ml (2tbsp) flour
500ml (18fl oz) whole milk
pinch of ground nutmeg
90ml (6tbsp) double cream
150g (5oz) prosciutto, finely chopped
4 spring onions, finely chopped
2 shallots or cloves of garlic, finely chopped
50g (2oz) Parmesan, grated
50g (2oz) Gruyère, grated
100g (12oz) short pasta, such as fusilli or penne
45ml (3tbsp) dry breadcrumbs
small handful parsley

Make a white sauce from the butter, flour and milk: melt the butter in a saucepan, then add the flour and stir constantly over a low heat for four-five minutes; now add the milk, a little at a time, stirring well to blend, and season halfway through with the nutmeg plus a good dose of salt and pepper. Leave to cool, then mix in the cream if using.

Meanwhile, preheat the oven to 200°C (400°F, Gas Mark 6). Stir all but a large spoonful of the cheese into the white sauce, and mix the rest with the breadcrumbs. Cook and drain the pasta, and toss it well with the prosciutto and the white sauce.

Decant into a buttered baking dish, top with the crumbs and cheese, and bake near the top of the oven till the interior is bubbling and the top nicely browned (around 25 minutes). Leave for a few minutes before serving.

Gratin 'Parmigiana'

This is just a gratin with Italian flavourings, and it's also good as a side dish. The tomato sauce can be from a jar if necessary.

300g (12oz) short pasta, such as fusilli or penne
1 clove garlic
butter
100ml (4fl oz) single cream
5ml (1tsp) dried oregano
225ml (8 fl oz) tomato sauce
150g (6oz) Italian mozzarella
60ml (4tbsp) fresh grated Parmesan

Preheat the oven to 180°C (350°F, Gas Mark 4). Boil a large pot of water for the pasta and get it cooking. Meanwhile, finely chop the garlic and liberally smear the inside of a gratin dish or shallow casserole dish with butter. Chop the mozzarella as finely as you can.

When the pasta is cooked, drain well and mix with the cream and oregano. Pour into the dish, top with the sauce and mozzarella, and finally sprinkle on the Parmesan. Bake in the upper third of the oven till the sauce is bubbling and the top browned (around 30 minutes). You can leave the dish for five-ten minutes before serving.

Cheat's Lasagne

A properly made lasagne, with home-made sheets of pasta and home-made tomato sauce and a mixture of meats (including chicken livers), is one of the greatest dishes in the world. It is certainly the greatest of oven-cooked pasta dishes. Unfortunately, it is also incredibly time-consuming. I never do it myself more than once or twice a year, and I couldn't in good conscience advise you to make one. If you do, the best recipes I've seen are to be found in Marcella Hazan's *The Essentials of Italian Cooklng* and Elizabeth David's *Italian Food*. What follows here is a cheat's version – pure and simple – which still takes a bit of time. But it tastes pretty good, and I make no apologies for presenting it as an alternative to authenticity for the busy cooks of today. The lasagne pasta must be of the kind that requires no pre-cooking. This is widely available; just check the label to make sure.

15ml (1tbsp) softened butter
15ml (1tbsp) plain flour
60ml (1 pint) milk
1 bay leaf
pinch of nutmeg, preferably freshly ground
1-2 cloves garlic
1 medium onion
15ml (1tbsp) extra virgin olive oil
375g (12 oz) best mince
1 packet mozzarella
extra butter for greasing the dish and dotting the top of the pasta
150-225g (6-8oz) dried lasagne, the no-pre-cook variety
l00ml (4 floz) tomato sauce, preferably home-made (see page 34)
around 60ml (4 tbsp) freshly grated Parmesan

First, make a béchamel sauce. Melt the butter over a low heat in a saucepan (nonstick is best) and stir in the flour with a wooden spoon. Cook, stirring constantly, for two-three minutes; the flour must not start to colour, but it must blend completely into the butter. Meanwhile, measure out the milk. Pour a little into the saucepan and stir constantly till it's absorbed. Add a little more and keep stirring till the extra milk's absorbed. Continue this process until the milk is all in; you can add it in larger doses towards the end. When all the milk is in, add the bay leaf and nutmeg, and turn the heat up a little so you get a steady, gentle simmer. The milk should not boil. Cook, stirring occasionally (and scraping the bottom of the pot for any stuck-on bits of flour) till the sauce is just thick enough to coat the back of your spoon. When it's reached this stage, leave to sit in the pan.

While the sauce is simmering, finely chop the onion and garlic. Heat the olive oil in a frying pan and cook them until they're very lightly coloured and very fragrant (around five minutes). Now add the mince, breaking up any big lumps, season with salt and pepper, and cook just until it's lost its raw colour (around five minutes). It does not need more cooking at this stage because it will cook thoroughly in the oven. Turn off the heat till it's needed.

While the mince is cooking, slice the mozzarella as thinly as you can manage. Generously butter the bottom and sides of a heavy baking-dish which has flat bottom and sides. Measure out the tomato sauce and Parmesan, and mix the sauce with the mince in the frying pan.

Preheat the oven to 200°C (400°F, Gas Mark 6). Put sheets of lasagne into the bottom of the baking dish, then put on a layer of sauce/mince, followed by a few pieces of mozzarella, followed by a small sprinkling of Parmesan. Lay on more sheets of lasagne, and repeat the procedure with the other ingredients. Continue till everything's used up, but try to make sure that the top layer has some of both cheeses on top. If the mozzarella has already run out, use more Parmesan. You can't really use too much Parmesan in this dish unless you spoon it on with a spade.

Now remove the bay leaf from the béchamel, and gently pour the sauce into the assembled lasagne. If possible, pour into one of the spaces at the edge of the dish so you don't splash the sprinkled Parmesan all over the place.

Season the top again with salt and pepper, dot generously with butter, and put in the oven on a shelf around two-thirds of the way up. The dish will need something between 30 and 60 minutes to cook. When it's done (which you can tell by seeing whether the inside is very liquid), let it rest out of the oven before serving. This needs nothing more than a green salad as a side dish. Serve with more grated Parmesan if you wish.

1-2-3 Baked Macaroni

This incredibly easy dish takes its name from the cookbook that inspired it: *Recipes 1-2-3* by Rozanne Gold (Grub Street). All the recipes in the book have just three ingredients, and while the original here was a version of Gratin Dauphinoise (made with potatoes), I have adapted it for use with pasta. The work involved is minimal, but the calories are maximal – so it's not something you would want to eat every day.

> *500g (1lb 2oz) short pasta such as penne or fusilli*
> *around 300ml (½ pint) single cream*
> *around 100-150g (4-6oz) Gruyère cheese*

Boil a large pot of water for the pasta and get it cooking, although you do not want to cook it fully at this stage. Remove from the heat and drain when it's around 1-2 minutes from being cooked. Meanwhile, preheat the oven to 180°C (350°F, Gas Mark 4); measure out the cream; and grate the cheese. Have ready a baking dish which holds the pasta comfortably.

When the pasta is done as specified above (i.e. still with a bit of crunch at the centre), drain it in the usual way and return to the pot. Pour in the cream plus a dose of salt and pepper, and turn the heat on to low. Cook the pasta, with regular stirring, for another 3-4 minutes – long enough to finish cooking but not long enough to make the pasta mushy. It should still be very *al dente*. Now tip it into the baking dish (no butter needed) and sprinkle the cheese over uniformly. Grind on a little more black pepper and bake in the upper third of the oven till the cream is bubbling and the top nicely browned (around 30-40 minutes). This needs nothing more than a side salad to go with it, and no extra cheese (though you could add some if you wish).